DOUBLE BILL

PAUL LEDOUX AND DAVID YOUNG

DOUBLE BILL

STILL DESIRE YOU

FIRE

PLAYWRIGHTS CANADA PRESS
TORONTO • CANADA

PLAYWRIGHTS CANADA PRESS
The Canadian Drama Publisher
215 Spadina Ave., Suite 230, Toronto, Ontario, Canada, M5T 2C7
phone 416.703.0013   fax 416.408.3402
orders@playwrightscanada.com • www.playwrightscanada.com

The publisher acknowledges the support of the Canadian taxpayers through the
Government of Canada Book Publishing Industry Development Program, the Canada
Council for the Arts, the Ontario Arts Council, and the Ontario Media Development
Corporation.

Production editor: Michael Petrasek
Cover designer: JLArt

LIBRARY AND ARCHIVES CANADA CATALOGUING IN PUBLICATION

Ledoux, Paul, 1949-
Double bill / Paul Ledoux and David Young.

Plays.
Contents: Still desire you - Fire.
ISBN 978-0-88754-817-8

I. Young, David, 1946- II. Title.

PS8573.E3439D69 2008   C812'.54   C2008-903216-0

*This book
was printed
on 100%
recycled stock.*

First edition: October 2008.
Printed and bound by AGMV Marquis at Quebec, Canada.

To director and collaborator Brian Richmond, who started the ball rolling and helped give birth to both these plays. Without his brilliance and tenacity they would not exist.

TABLE OF CONTENTS

PLAYWRIGHTS' NOTES

Both of these plays generated out of our interest in the interpenetrating relationships between carnal desire, spiritual love, media and popular music.

In *Still Desire You* (a fresh adaptation of *I Love You, Anne Murray*, first produced in the 1980s) we tell the story of a lonely fan's obsession with a pop star. The play deals with issues that are central to the growing malaise of celebrity culture in our society. The music business inundates us with media-driven gossip, much of it stage managed to help create the branding of a star and the illusory sense of personal connection that cements a fan base. The commercial objective is to bind fan and performer in a "private world" that seems as real, personal and intimate as a love affair.

All of us treasure certain songs because they have a personal connection. String these songs together and they form a private soundtrack for our interior lives—who we were, who we are and who we want to be. For some fans, innocent fantasies about their connection to the performer behind the song can become real and dangerous obsessions.

Such is the story of David Stuart, a fundamentally decent man on trial for "the crime of loving a girl" who happens to be a pop icon. *Still Desire You* explores the slippery slope of a fan's delusions and, in the process, indicts the star-making machinery behind our communal obsession with celebrity.

Fire is a play about searching for salvation with your head, your heart and your groin. It grew out of our fascination with the extraordinary relationship between Pentecostal Christianity and the birth of rock and roll. The early pioneers of rock music stole the religious fire found in the churches of the American South and started a secular and sexual conflagration that changed the world. But the early legends of rock, all of whom began their careers singing in church, often found themselves in conflict with their deeply held religious beliefs—their desire for a higher spiritual existence constantly at war with the carnal immediacy that is the essence of rock and roll.

Driven by the transistorized, supercharged media explosion of the fifties this raw and emotive form of popular music had unprecedented power in a rapidly evolving consumerist society. At the same time, it triggered a political backlash that continues to find amplification in the internet era.

In developing *Fire*, our understanding of the issues was informed by the uniquely intertwined lives of Jerry Lee Lewis and his cousin Reverend Jimmy Swaggart.

Jerry Lee's meteoric rise to superstardom led to scandal when it was revealed that he had married his thirteen-year-old cousin. Despite his subsequent fall from grace, run-ins with the law and personal tragedies, Lewis remained the quintessential rock-and-roll rebel and a model for a generation of baby boomers who, in the sixties, triggered an explosive social revolution. Jerry Lee's fire lit that fuse.

Meanwhile, Jimmy Swaggart built a ministry that helped define the new universe of televangelism. Along with a handful of other television preachers, he inadvertently identified a vast conservative constituency, the "silent majority." The American far right, reeling from the media savvy attacks of the left, now saw the corrupting power of media being turned on its head. Ultra-conservative ideologues formed political alliances with the evangelical churches. By the Reagan era, the term "right-wing fundamentalism" had become central to American political discourse. The fire in Swaggart's sermons lit this political fuse.

We like to think of these two plays as the A and B sides of an old 45. Both explore the unique power of popular music, be it gospel, pop or rock and roll. Both explore the corrosive nature of fame. Finally, both are about the struggle to find spiritual meaning within the maelstrom of a media-driven culture that careens along the edge of chaos and is still just picking up speed.

Paul Ledoux, David Young
March 17, 2008

STILL DESIRE YOU

WITH THE MUSIC OF MELANIE DOANE

Still Desire You premiered in September 2007 at Western Canada Theatre, Kamloops, BC, in a co-production with Alberta Theatre Projects, Calgary, Alberta with the following company:

ROSE McKAY	Erin McGrath
DAVID STUART	Christopher Hunt
JUDGE	Alec Willows
CROWN, ADAM CLAY	John Wright
DR. C.G. RAND, GINO,	
JONES, RICK, SANDY	John Murphy
ELLEN SMALL,	
DR. KIM DOWNEY	Sarah Donald
CLERK, COP	Tim Williams

Director: Paul Ledoux
Musical Director: Tim Williams
Set & Lighting Design: Terry Gunvordahl
Costume Design: Juli Elkiw

CHARACTERS

DAVID STUART: (early forties) an articulate, highly intelligent loner from rural Nova Scotia

ROSE MCKAY: (early to mid-thirties) beautiful young pop superstar

CROWN: (forties) a slightly pompous, ambitious prosecutor (doubles Clay, band)

JUDGE: a sympathetic character with a wry sense of humour (could play in band)

DR. C.G. RAND: prissy psychiatrist (doubles Jones, Rick, Gino, band)

SGT. JONES: surly cop with a notebook where his heart should be

ELLEN SMALL: Rose's head of publicity

ADAM CLAY: Rose's husband, a slick record producer with some rough edges

RICK PHILLIPS: speedy little autograph hound

GINO: inmate at a hospital for the criminally insane

DR. KIM DOWNEY: young psychiatrist with a social conscience

COURT CLERK, COP: played by the musical director

*Additional minor characters are all doubled by cast or band members.

The play can be performed by a cast of seven very versatile actor/musicians. However, in some cases it may be necessary to hire additional musicians.

SET NOTES

The action primarily takes place in a courtroom; however, during the course of the play Stuart breaks the fourth wall to speak directly to the audience. He also tries to reconstruct the details of his relationship with Rose in a series of memory scenes taking place in many locations; his shop, clubs, arenas, backstage, at dressing-room doors, at a funeral. Additional action takes place in a hospital for the criminally insane.. There is virtually no time for set changes so the play requires an extremely flexible unit set.

ACT ONE

SCENE ONE: WHAT KIND OF MAN

In the blackout we hear "ding" and then music under: "Never Doubt I Love" played like an achingly beautiful Scottish aire on solo fiddle.

Lighting effect up: ROSE McKAY enters far upstage, a silhouette against a fishing village backdrop. DAVID STUART stands by the defence desk carrying an old leather briefcase packed with paper. He pauses, listens, and looks off in her direction.

ROSE   *In an age of troubles*
In an age of uncertainty
In an age of dwindling hope
You still have me

No matter where you are
No matter how far from home
No matter if you're lost
You still have me

> *Vocal count in for song. The band hits hard. A spotlight on ROSE as she dances downstage singing "Wilma or a Betty Man." The band add backing vocals on the refrains.*

> *STUART unpacks his briefcase during the song, his attention constantly drawn to ROSE. It's like he's remembering one of her early music videos.*

This love is so new
And I wanna know everything about you
Like what do you wear to bed
Do you think Elvis is dead?
I wanna know everything
That's going on in your head

Are you a Wilma or a Betty man?
Do you drive a Mercedes or a Trans Am?
Do you have a single malt or a beer in your hand?
Will you love me like no other can?
(What kinda man...)

I wanna know
(What kinda man...)
I wanna know.

Do you like when I touch your hair?
Are you wearing boxers under there?
Tell me, who was your first kiss?
Did it feel like this?
Who makes it on your desert-island list?

Are you a Wilma or a Betty man?
Do you drive a Mercedes or a Trans Am?
Do you have a single malt or a beer in your hand?
Will you love me like no other can?
(What kinda man...)
I wanna know.
(What kinda man...)
I wanna know

> The tone shifts for a moment as ROSE seems to see
> STUART. Slowly she walks towards him, finally leaning
> over his desk.

The more of you you let me see
The stronger I know my love will be
I was trying to understand
So come on show me what kinda man
Oh yeah

> For a moment she's singing directly to him and then she
> spins away, back into the number.

So, what do you wear to bed?
Do you think Elvis is dead?
I wanna know everything
That's going on in your head
Are you a Wilma or a Betty man?
Do you drive a Mercedes or a Trans Am?
Do you have a single malt or a beer in your hand?
Will you love me like no other can?
(What kinda man...)
I wanna know
(What kinda man...)

I wanna know
(What kinda man…)
I wanna know
I WANNA KNOW

> *ROSE and the band exit. Drum/gavel rap begins*
> *courtroom scene.*

SCENE TWO: THE SUBSTANCE OF THE CASE

CLERK Order in the court. In the matter of David Stuart, Judge William Richmond presiding. All rise.

JUDGE David Charles Stuart, you are charged with breach of probation in that on or about April 23, 2006, in the Municipality of Metropolitan Toronto, you did wilfully violate a probation order of the Ontario Court of Justice. To wit, not to attend at the offices of Rose McKay. How do you plead to this charge?

STUART I plead not guilty.

JUDGE The Crown may proceed.

CROWN Your Honour, the accused, David Stuart, suffers, for lack of a better word, from an ongoing 'infatuation' with the singer Rose McKay. As a result of this infatuation, he's been in and out of court for the last three years.

JUDGE Yes, I have the arrest record before me. And all of these charges relate to this… Ms. McKay.

CROWN It's Rose McKay, Your Honour… *(JUDGE draws a blank)* …of singing fame.

JUDGE I see.

> *STUART looks out at the audience.*

STUART Salt water in our blood, that's the bond. You see, Rose and I both come from seafaring people. Father to father, son to son, for five generations our families have "gone down to the sea in ships" and fought for a living out there.

JUDGE   I see that Mr. Stuart is from Nova Scotia.

CROWN   Yes, Your Honour. As is Ms. McKay.

STUART   I've been arrested eight times for being in love with her.

CROWN   He feels that is part of a "special bond" between them.

STUART   It's true... I love her.

CROWN   I think his record pretty much establishes the fact that Mr. Stuart has a habit of ignoring court orders in this matter. It's all there in your documents, sir.

The JUDGE leafs through court documents.

STUART   If Rose were here she could clear this whole thing up in about three seconds flat, but that's not her way. It never has been. It's crazy, but who knows, maybe everyone who falls in love is a little bit crazy. See, when two people fall in love they're in each other's head all day long, no matter what kind of distance is between them. Love arcs like electricity... across a city... across an ocean... like a halo around the world.

JUDGE   Yes, interesting. Could we move on to the charge at hand?

STUART   Now, here's what I don't understand. For nearly ten years I have been in correspondence with Rose. I have sent her gifts. I have seen her face to face whenever our schedules permitted. For ten years she not only welcomed my interest, she *encouraged* it. Then one day, out of the blue, I'm arrested and thrown in jail.

CROWN   The substance of the charge is simple, Your Honour. On April 23, 2006, Mr. Stuart went to Rose McKay's office and left her a letter. This was in direct violation of a court order prohibiting Mr. Stuart from communicating with Ms. McKay in any way or attending at the homes or offices of herself, her family or her employees.

STUART   I was forty-three years old and had never so much as picked up a parking ticket. Suddenly I was trapped in a legal revolving door.

CROWN Miss Ellen Small, Ms. McKay's executive assistant, took the letter and called the police.

STUART I reach out towards Rose and I'm arrested. Again. The same charge. The same arresting officer.

CROWN Mr. Stuart was arrested at Pearson International Airport.

STUART Even the same prosecutor, Mr. T.L. Broilman, a big feeling, publicity-grubbing Toronto fool. Of course, the press eats it up. And the result of this circus? I end up in the Willows Mental Health Centre, Canada's most famous prison for the criminally insane—for doing what? For writing a girl a love letter.

CROWN When he was arrested, Mr. Stuart told the arresting officer, "When it comes to my relationship with Rose McKay, the police make no more sense than arseholes snapping in the wind."

SCENE THREE: I OBJECT

STUART *(stands)* I object, Your Honour.

JUDGE One moment. Mr. Stuart?

STUART I would just like to inform the Court that my statement grew out of an exchange of insults between myself and the arresting officer—a Sergeant Jones. He's one of those fellas who's always got to get ugly. He called me down something awful. I responded in kind.

JUDGE "Snapping in the wind."

STUART The phrase suggests a lack of intelligence, Your Honour.

JUDGE Don't worry, Mr. Stuart. Colourful criticism of police intelligence is not a criminal offence. At least not in my court. Do you have counsel?

STUART I'm defending myself, sir.

JUDGE You realize the seriousness of this matter, Mr. Stuart?

STUART I do, Your Honour.

JUDGE You are facing a jail sentence here.

STUART   For personal reasons I prefer to defend myself.

JUDGE   Just as long as you know a lawyer can be made available to you.

STUART   Yes, thank you, Your Honour. Based on my previous encounters with Mr. Broilman, I should do just fine.

JUDGE   Good. You have everything you need for your defence?

STUART   Yes, Your Honour.

JUDGE   Let's proceed.

CROWN   Yes, Your Honour, it's my intention to...

STUART   Your Honour, if I might add—

JUDGE   Yes, Mr. Stuart?

STUART   I just want to add, about this "snapping in the wind" incident, that in general I'm very sympathetic towards police officers. My difficulty with this officer is part of an ongoing situation, which I will bring to the Court's attention in due course.

JUDGE   We'll look forward to that, Mr. Stuart.

STUART   There's a very good case to be made for the fact that I'm on trial here for being in love with Rose McKay.

JUDGE   Let me assure you, that is not how the charge reads. Mr. Broilman?

CROWN   Thank you, Your Honour. Mr. Stuart's remarks have brought us very nicely to my first, and I hope only, witness in these proceedings. I would like to call Dr. C.G. Rand.

STUART   I object, Your Honour.

CROWN   It is my belief that Dr. Rand will be able to show the Court that there is every reason to believe Mr. Stuart's mental condition makes him unfit to stand trial.

JUDGE   Do you understand Dr. Rand's role in these proceedings, Mr. Stuart?

STUART   All too well, Your Honour. I've been through all of this before. Last year, on the basis of Dr. Rand's testimony,

I was committed to the Willows, the hospital for the criminally insane where Dr. Rand works. After some months of incarceration, my appeal on this committal came before the provincial mental health board of review and I was released. As the board has already overturned Dr. Rand's diagnosis, his presence here is irrelevant.

CROWN Your Honour, while it is true that the board of review did decertify Mr. Stuart, that does not mean that in the board's opinion his actions are those of a sane man.

STUART Then, Your Honour, I wonder if Mr. Broilman could explain what it does mean?

CROWN It means that, in their opinion, the severity or type of mental illness present at that time was not sufficient to warrant further incarceration.

STUART So I was crazy, but not crazy enough to be locked up?

JUDGE In essence, I believe that's what the Crown is suggesting.

STUART Sounds like half the people in Toronto.

CROWN Your Honour, I'm sure Dr. Rand could illuminate this issue for us all.

JUDGE Mr. Stuart, at this stage in the proceedings the Crown has the right to raise this matter; however, you will be given every opportunity to cross-examine the doctor.

STUART Thank you, Your Honour.

SCENE FOUR: MR. STUART IS INSANE

CROWN Dr. C.G. Rand, please.

CLERK Dr. C.G. Rand.

> *RAND takes the stand. We follow the proceedings as he is sworn in but listen to STUART.*

STUART Here we go again. This gentleman has a mind like a cookie cutter and the emotional maturity of SpongeBob SquarePants. He's got one answer for everything that has to do with the workings of the human heart: look it up in

CROWN Dr. Rand, are you able to tell the Court what, in your view, Mr. Stuart is suffering from?

RAND Mr. Stuart suffers from a classic case of erotic paranoia.

JUDGE looks up, he's been reading a report.

JUDGE What? What was that?

CROWN Erotic paranoia.

RAND It's a textbook case, really. The patient believes that some woman whom he may have casually seen or met is in love with him. He writes her affectionate letters and perhaps poems. Her failure to respond in kind is intended solely to test his love.

SCENE FIVE: A DOWN-TO-EARTH BEGINNING

STUART Did you see the way everyone perked up when he said the magic word? EROTIC. I looked it up online, it's from the Greek, eros, meaning "the drive towards higher forms of being and relationship." But look at them, like a bunch of blagarding boys clamouring over a girlie magazine in the back corner of a schoolyard. They turn me into whatever it is they fear about themselves. Fact is, this whole thing began in about as down-to-earth a way as you can imagine. It was my thirty-sixth birthday.

Musicians underscore monologue. Drums, flute and guitar create hints of the soft sound of gulls, shifting ice, water lapping on the shore. Lights shift. We are in STUART's workshop.

I was in the shop, like always, working. I've got a tight little shed on a wharf with a fine view up the gut to the open sea. I put in a nice sheet of thermo-pane across the front—gives you the feeling you're right out there in it. Of course, The FOG Shop looks completely traditional from roadside. Fog. F.O.G.—it's an acronym for "From Old

Guys." My father used to say, "There's not much worth havin' I didn't get from some old guy had her further back." And I guess that's about right. But you can't just run before the storm, no sir. The trick is to hold onto what's right and still survive in a modern world. Easier said than done. Oh, I played the tourist game with the best of them. Established an "internet presence" and all that but... it's the shop I love. The smell of fresh-planed oak and salt sea, all part of one thing.... Somehow I still couldn't put those two worlds together inside my heart.

It was late November. End of day, the light just falling. Ice barely crusting along the shore and a dusting of snow that spoke of what was to come. My thirty-sixth birth-day.... I've spent the day alone, steaming thin strips of cherry wood, bending them to shape over handmade moulds, perfect ovals in six different sizes. Shaker-style nesting boxes built the old way. I can sell as many as I can turn out come Christmas.

I still remember the smell of Old Spice, a little present I bought for myself in town, *(sings old jingle)* "fresh as the breeze" ...and with that aroma, the exact thought I have as I reach to turn on the radio...

I'm thinking about my place in the world. Thirty-six years old and where am I? A man working in an old fish shed, on an empty road, in a near deserted village, looking out across the empty bay to the place where sea and fog become one. Out there, one lonely gull up high—a speck against the grey sky. And it's like I'm up there with him, looking down on that little shed with my life inside it.

> *Live underscoring fades into pre-recorded radio sound effects. STUART tunes in a series of stations. Static, stations, bursts of pop music, news, etc.*

ANNOUNCER   *(offstage)* From Block Island to Cape Sable. Storm warning in effect...

ANNOUNCER 2   *(offstage)* Weather bomb...

ANNOUNCER 3   *(offstage)* ...hurricane-related casualties in western Florida...

ANNOUNCER 4   (*offstage*) Refused to comment upon...

ANNOUNCER   (*offstage*) High at 2:26 and 14:50 Atlantic Standard Time. Low tides at...

STUART   I see myself inside that great stillness and think... this is it, buddy, this is as good as she gets. The tide under the wharf rising and falling with the moon, the tilt of the earth on its axis as we journey 'round the sun. Season upon season... until she floods over or blows away.

DJ   (*offstage*) I think we're going to hear great things from this little girl from Margaree. Here's Rose McKay.

SCENE SIX: SHE'S LIKE A SWALLOW

> *A clear voice rings out singing "She's Like a Swallow" a capella. ROSE appears on a low riser with members of her band. She's dressed simply. This is the very beginning of her breakout. As she plays and sings, STUART is enraptured by the song.*

ROSE   *She's like the swallow that flies so high*
She's like the river that never runs dry
She's like the sunshine on the lee shore
I love my love and love is no more

> *Music in.*

'Twas out in the garden this fair maid did go
Picking the beautiful primrose
The more she plucked the more she pulled
Until she got her apron full

> *Under STUART's monologue, ROSE plays the fiddle, trading musical lines with the guitar player.*

STUART   I always felt like no one ever got who I was, that I tried to stand for something... bigger than myself. Not so long ago Nova Scotia boasted the third-largest fleet in the world. Wooden ships and iron men, eh? And my family built the hulls and crafted the lines of the finest fleet of sailing vessels anybody had ever seen. I worked the family yard alongside my brothers most of my life, until the old man passed and they decided to start laying up with fibreglass. That was the end of it for me. Somebody somewhere had to try and hold onto traditions that made us who we were. That's how it was with my father.

ROSE   *She's like the swallow that flies so high*
She's like the river that never runs dry
She's like the sunshine on the lee shore
I love my love and love is no more
I love my love and love is no more

> *Second fiddle break. ROSE takes centre stage. STUART continues to speak to ROSE. She can't hear him.*

STUART   You took that old song I'd heard and sung a thousand times and you brought it to life again, made it real and important and alive. You were taking our music and doing what I was trying to do inside my own life. And it worked.

> *Song ends and ROSE begins to exit.*

I fell for you at that very moment and I knew I would never feel that alone again.

> *ROSE looks back at STUART — as their eyes meet there's a "ding," then she exits. Lights shift to courtroom.*

SCENE SEVEN: MR. STUART CAN DEFEND HIMSELF

CROWN   So, in summing up, would you say that Mr. Stuart's condition must inevitably deteriorate?

RAND   Without treatment, yes. I have no idea what he may do next.

CROWN   No further questions, Your Honour.

JUDGE   Mr. Stuart, you may cross-examine Dr. Rand.

STUART   Thank you, Your Honour. Dr. Rand, it would seem that crucial to your whole argument is the delusional aspect of my mental state. Is that right?

RAND   That is the primary symptom, yes.

STUART   What am I deluded about?

RAND   That this relationship between you and Rose McKay exists.

STUART   I see. And what constitutes a relationship between two people, Dr. Rand?

RAND   Well, I would guess a mutual acceptance of the fact that a relationship exists.

STUART   You mean I would have to be asked if I believe there is a relationship between Rose McKay and myself, and then she would have to be asked?

RAND   That's the whole problem, David. There has been no mutual response on her part.

STUART   You know that isn't true, Clarence. You know from previous appearances that I have produced proof of her response... for instance, this letter and picture sent to me by Rose McKay.

> *STUART takes a picture from his briefcase and gives it to RAND.*

Could you please read the inscription on the photo for the Court?

Christopher Hunt in Western Canada Theatre's and Alberta Theatre Projects' premiere production of *Still Desire You*. Photo by Murray Mitchell.

RAND   But a person in her position probably gets letters from a large number of—

JUDGE   The inscription please, Dr. Rand.

RAND   "Keep in touch, Rose." But this is the kind of picture Ms. McKay would send out to all her fans. Does that mean she has a "close" relationship with each and every person she responds to?

STUART   Dr. Rand, I would suggest that she does indeed have a relationship with those people. However, I would note that you have added the word "close" to our discussion.

RAND   You have always insisted that the relationship is intimate.

STUART   Oh, so now you are adding "intimacy" to our relationship.

RAND   All I'm trying to say is...

STUART   You didn't suggest my delusional system was based on intimacy when I asked you to define your terms, Dr. Rand. Why are you trying to confuse the issue now?

RAND   I am not trying to confuse the issue. All I am saying is that your relationship with Ms. McKay is the same kind of relationship she has with thousands of other fans who correspond with her.

STUART   Your Honour, a moment ago Dr. Rand claimed I should be committed to a hospital for the criminally insane because I am deluded in my belief that I have a relationship with Rose McKay. He now admits that, in fact, I have had a relationship—perhaps casual, perhaps not—but nevertheless, a relationship. Having lost that point he then falls back on innuendo, suggesting I believe I have an "intimate" relationship with Rose when, in fact, I have suggested no such thing in court today. I have no more questions for this witness. Clearly, he is contradicting himself and, in view of the decision by the review board that I'm as safe to walk the streets as the next fellow, I ask the Court to find that I am fit to stand trial.

Time hangs as JUDGE considers the request.

JUDGE   Well, Mr. Stuart, you are clearly able to defend yourself.

CROWN   Your Honour, Mr. Stuart has in the past freely admitted that he believes Rose McKay is madly in love with him!

STUART   Your Honour, I'm on trial for breaking probation. My dramatically publicized "love" for Rose McKay is not the real issue here, as you stated earlier.

JUDGE   Quite so, Mr. Stuart. Dr. Rand may step down, but at any time during this trial if I decide that the issue of your mental health is substantive, I may recall the doctor.

RAND exits.

STUART   Yes. Thank you, Your Honour.

JUDGE   Let us proceed.

SCENE EIGHT: THE SALES PITCH

CROWN   Miss Ellen Small, please.

CLERK   Miss Ellen Small.

STUART   Ellen Small manages Rose's office. For years I thought she was one of the sweetest people I'd ever talked to. I remember the first time I phoned. Rose's second CD had been released. "Saltwater" was on the radio all the time—and I just couldn't get Rose out of my mind. I'd go to her web-site and read her tour journal and she always answered all the questions posted. I requested a photo. There it was in the mail. I framed it and hung it up over the cash and... there's a handwritten inscription on that picture. It says, "Keep in touch." So, one day I just picked up the phone and called...

> *STUART pulls out a telephone and dials. Lights down on court and up on the offices of Saltwater Productions. A phone and a laptop sit on a desk. A party is in progress in the back room: riotous singing of "The Mermaid of Port Mouton," which fades up and down under the*

> scene. Note: use only as much of the song as is needed to underscore the scene.

BAND   *Now I'm a longliner from a fishing town*
That is known as Port Mouton
But I left the sea some years ago
And I won't be going back soon
For I fell in love one foggy night
In the lea of a terrible gale
With a bonny lass who, lads, alas
Was a mermaid with a salty tail

> *ELLEN SMALL enters with an ice bucket as the phone rings.*

SMALL   Fellas! Can you keep it down a bit!!

BAND   *(softer, under SMALL) I will ne'er forget when our lips first met*
And I loved her from fluke to fin
But come the break of day, anchors away
I lost her for I cannot swim

SMALL   Saltwater Productions, Ellen Small speaking, can I help you?

STUART   Ah… yes… this is David Stuart from Blue Rocks?

SMALL   *(checks phone for caller ID)* Nova Scotia?

STUART   That's right. You know The Rocks?

SMALL   I know Nova Scotia, that's for sure. Area code 902.

STUART   Of course you do—I mean you'd have to…. Anyway, actually… ah… I wrote Rose a little while ago and she wrote me back and so I thought… that, you know, maybe I should phone and see how she's doing.

> *The dynamic of the party noise increases as ADAM CLAY enters, then becomes soft again. As if a door has opened and closed behind him. Song continues under.*

CLAY   *(spoken)* Ellen, we are sooo out of ice. Not cool.

BAND   *Now the seas rolled on and the months passed by*
Till one evening off Banquero
I heard a song so beautiful

> *That I climbed out the yardarm pole*
> *And there she blew off the starboard bow*
> *Wearin' nothin' but a cockle shell*
> *And though I could not swim, I jumped right in*
> *And sank beneath the salty swell*

SMALL   She's doing just fine, Mr. Stuart. Thanks for the call.

STUART   Is she... is she there?

SMALL   No, I'm sorry, she's gone... to rehearsal. But she'll be sorry she missed you.

> *An instrumental musical break featuring ROSE on fiddle.*

CLAY   Business, Ellen m'darlin'?

SMALL   Do you mind holding? *(covers phone)* Just a fan. "Down home."

CLAY   Well Lord-liftin-Jesus, let's see this fan database you're always bragging about in action. Unleash the hounds!

> *She enters a command on the computer.*

That's fast. What's the name?

STUART   Hello?

SMALL   Yes, she'll be some sorry she missed you, Mr. Stuart.

> *CLAY types.*

STUART   She sent me a couple of lovely notes in response to my letters.

SMALL   Yes, I think I remember. You're the...

CLAY   He builds dories!

SMALL   You're a dory builder!

STUART   That's right!

CLAY   Work it, girl. Work it.

SMALL   Yes. Well, that makes you kind of special, doesn't it. For a girl like Rose. She misses home something awful, you know.

STUART   Yes, I've been listening to the new song a lot.

SMALL   *(sings) Send me some salt water.*

STUART   It's great, isn't it? In fact, I almost sent her some.

SMALL   Some what?

STUART   Salt water. There's a whole bay-full right out my front door.

SMALL   Maybe you should.

STUART   Should what?

SMALL   Send her some salt water.

STUART   You think she'd...

SMALL   I think she'd love it.

STUART   Well, gosh, if you think so I'll send her some.

SMALL   Sure, you might just start a trend, eh? *(covers phone)* He's going to send her some salt water.

CLAY   You are a genius!

ROSE & BAND   *(bridge) So it's down below with a yo ho ho*
To her kingdom far beneath the sea
Davy Jones might soon be pickin' my bones
But her song it was that sweet to me
And she held me tight with all her might
As we spun upon an azure rip
Imagine my surprise when I opened my eyes
And I was back aboard my ship

STUART   Gee, sounds like you're having a bit of a do over there.

SMALL   Yes, well, it's just a little bon voyage celebration. Rose is going out on tour next week.

ROSE & BAND   *(continues softly under) Now I sit on a dune 'neath*
the Mouton moon
And ponder my time 'neath the sea
And some starry nights, to my fright and delight
(stop) A dolphin splashes by who looks like me

CLAY   Is he coming to the show? Maybe we could get some publicity stills.

SMALL   Maybe you can make one of the shows. She'd love to see you.

STUART   You know I've never seen her in person. Is she coming down home?

SMALL   Not this time, I'm afraid. She's got a solo concert in Vancouver this weekend and then she joins Lilith Fair for the summer tour, mostly American dates.

STUART   Vancouver. Well, that's a ways from here. I don't think it's likely, see, I'd have to fly to get there.

SMALL   You sure as heck couldn't walk.

STUART   I guess most people would think nothing of flying to Vancouver to see Rose...

SMALL   *(covers phone)* Boring!

CLAY   Give me that!

SMALL   Adam!

CLAY   Mr. Stuart!

STUART   Yes?

CLAY   Congratulations. You're the thousandth caller.

STUART & SMALL   Thousandth caller?

CLAY   This week. And to express our gratitude to all the fans out there this week the thousandth caller wins free tickets to Rose's show in Vancouver, and a chance to meet the Saltwater Girl herself up close and personal. ALL you've got to do is show up!!

SMALL   *(whispers)* Mr. Clay, you are shameless.

STUART   Hello?

SMALL   Keep in touch!

    Music stops. The line goes dead.

STUART   Fly to Vancouver. Vancouver. *(STUART shakes his head. What madness. He looks at the audience.)* I sat there in the shop trying to measure the strength of my feelings. I was ramping up for the mail-order season with a half hundred projects scattered about. Taking time off now made no sense but...

Underscoring. Intro to "Saltwater."

I sipped my tea and looked at Rose's picture smiling down at me... for an instant it seemed like the only sane thing to do was to forget the whole thing... then... at that precise moment... there she was on the radio.

> *ROSE enters and sings "Saltwater." We might be looking at a simply staged, romantic music video from early in her career. As she sings she sits and pulls out a letter and reads it.*

ROSE *Said goodbye for the summer*
That to my surprise
Has turned into a lifetime
If I had known then that
You were the price I'd pay
I would have stayed
So glad I didn't know
But I miss the sea
And I miss seeing you so

Send me some salt water
Send me some salt water
Send me some salt water
And I will cry my salty tears back to you

Time is slipping and your face is fading
But your voice is clear
I hear the words you spoke
Those final words
As if you were here

> *STUART joins in, at first half speaking and singing. Then he sings, getting swept up in the song. ROSE crosses towards him. For a moment the song becomes a duet.*

ROSE & STUART *Don't go, I think I love you*

ROSE   But I miss the sea
             And I miss seeing you so...
             So, send me some salt water

ROSE & STUART   Send me some salt water

ROSE   Send me some salt water
             And I will cry my salty tears back to you

             Oh Bluenose sailed away
             Leaving me behind
             All I have to hold on to
             Is the silver silhouette on a dime
             The place I used to call mine
             Is now where I vacation from time to time

> Lights around STUART shift as he sings again—
> beautifully.

ROSE & STUART   Farewell to Nova Scotia, the sea-bound coast
             May your mountains dark and dreary be
             For when I am far away
             From the briny ocean tossed
             Will you heave a sigh for me,

ROSE   Oh but I miss the sea

ROSE & STUART   And I miss seeing you so...
             Send me some salt water
             Send me some salt water
             Send me some salt water
             And I will cry my salty tears

             I will cry my salty tears
             I will cry my salty tears back to you
             I will cry my salty tears
             I will cry my salty tears

ROSE   I will cry my salty tears to you

> ROSE exits.

STUART   Somehow that song made it seem that my "prize" was
             more like a personal invitation.

Lights shift back to court. SMALL is being sworn in. She sits in the witness box.

SCENE NINE: A LOVE LETTER

SMALL   Ellen Small. Saltwater Productions.

CROWN   Now, Miss Small, you are employed by Saltwater Productions, Ms. McKay's personal management company. You were on the Saltwater premises on April 23, 2006, is that correct?

SMALL   Yes, I was walking through the reception area and looked up and saw Mr. Stuart standing by the office door.

CROWN   Yes, and how were you able to see him?

SMALL   The door is made out of smoked glass.

CROWN   All right. And what did you do after you saw him?

SMALL   Well, I was frightened at first, but finally I went to the door, opened it and Mr. Stuart... he spoke first, said, "I'd like to leave a personal message for Ms. McKay." And I said, "Fine." I accepted the envelope from him, closed the door, read the letter and telephoned the police.

CROWN   Good. Now, Miss Small, can you identify this object for the court?

SMALL   *(taking the envelope)* Yes. That's the letter Mr. Stuart gave me. See, it says right here: "Rose McKay. Personal."

CROWN   Your Honour. *(hands the letter to the JUDGE, then crosses to STUART)* Copy for you Mr. Stuart. No more questions.

STUART   *(to audience)* Letters have played a special part in our relationship. For a long time it was enough to post to her website, but as things progressed it was clear that the internet was just way too public a venue to express feelings we wanted to share. A personal letter... a letter has real emotional weight.

JUDGE   Mr. Stuart?

STUART   Yes, Your Honour, thank you. Miss Small, you've said I frighten you.

SMALL   That is correct.

STUART   Why? Have I ever done anything that has caused you to be afraid of me?

SMALL   I'm frightened when you come to the office.

STUART   Yes, I understand. But why?

SMALL   Because you keep coming back regardless of court orders.

STUART   But, aside from the issue of court orders, what personal conduct have I displayed that causes you to be afraid of me?

JUDGE   Excuse me, Mr. Stuart, I'm having trouble following your argument. "Personal conduct"? How does this relate to the case?

STUART   I'm trying to establish two things, Your Honour. First, that there has never been any indication that my actions gave anybody cause to be afraid of me. Second, that there has been no representation made by office staff that anything I wished to leave was unacceptable.

JUDGE   I see. Well, because you are defending yourself I will allow you some latitude.

STUART   Thank you, Your Honour. I would like to ask the witness if she has ever personally declined a message to Rose.

SMALL   I have never personally declined a message from you, Mr. Stuart. I'd be afraid to.

STUART   But why?

SMALL   Because I think you're crazy.

STUART   So, you saw this lunatic lurking out in the hall but you didn't call the police, you unlock the door, take a letter from this very, very frightening madman and say, "She's in."

SMALL   I didn't say that, Mr. Stuart.

STUART   Was she in?

SMALL   That has nothing to do with—

STUART She was in there and the reason you took that letter from me instead of calling the police was that Rose told you to, didn't she?

SMALL The police said we should…

STUART The police! The police weren't called until after Rose read my letter and knew I was leaving town, with or without her.

SMALL That's not what happened.

STUART Then why was I arrested at the airport? Could it be because Rose can't get all this public attention focused on her and me if I'm back home?

SMALL It's because she's afraid of you!

STUART Then why doesn't she act like she's afraid of me? Why does she take my letters?

SMALL You have no idea what it's like to be afraid of someone, Mr. Stuart.

STUART No further questions.

SCENE TEN: LOVE TESTS YOUR FAITH

STUART *(to audience)* That woman could send me to the jail or worse—blanket my sails proper—and she sits up there telling me I have no idea what it's like to be afraid of someone. *(chuckles)* I'll tell you, "the mercy of the Court" has taught me a thing or two about fear.

Of course, all of this is nothing compared to how I felt the first time I went to see Rose. I was scared to death!

> *Band sets up stage area on an upstage riser. Two bar stools are set downstage.*

But love always tests your faith. If you don't believe in something bigger than yourself… you fail. I took eight hundred dollars I didn't have out of my bank account and drove to the airport.

The next thing I knew, I was in Gastown, Vancouver,
British Columbia, sitting in a bar called The Town Pump.

SCENE ELEVEN: AWAKE

*Applause. Lights up on ROSE, now starting to have
a more contemporary look and sound. She sings
"Goliath," the band sings backup. CLAY, playing rhythm
guitar, also directs the band. He's clearly in charge.*

ROSE   Thank you! Here's one from the new album! Called
"Goliath"!

*(sings) I've been sleeping under the beanstalk
And I've been dreaming of something big
I don't know how but I could swear
I'm on my way somewhere*

*(Awake the giant) Awake
(Awake, awake) Awake
Hey Goliath oh, you're no bigger
You're no bigger than me
Hey Goliath oh, you're no bigger
You're no bigger than me*

*I know I've got something inside of me
Just like I know you've got something inside of you
It might be hard but if we dare
We're on our way somewhere*

*(Awake the giant) Awake
(Awake, awake) Awake
Hey Goliath oh, you're no bigger
You're no bigger than me
Hey Goliath oh, you're no bigger
You're no bigger than me*

> *ROSE grabs her mic and walks downstage, playing the
> audience. She picks STUART out and sings the bridge to
> him.*

*Say the words you have swallowed
See the visions in your mind's eye*

Do what you feel in your heart
Awake the giant in you

I've been waiting for a signal
For something to tell me everything's all right
But now I see it's up to me
No one else can fight this fight

> *ROSE goes back on stage and finishes the song, throwing her arm up in a power salute, which STUART, now standing and swept up in the song, shyly emulates.*

(Awake the giant) Awake
(Awake, awake) Awake
Hey Goliath oh, you're no bigger
You're no bigger than me
Hey Goliath oh, you're no bigger
You're no bigger than me
Hey Goliath oh, you're no bigger
You're no bigger than me
Hey Goliath oh, you're no bigger
You're no bigger than me

Thank you! Good night!

> *ROSE takes a bow and exits. The song finishes on an extended coda under STUART.*

STUART "Awake the giant in you." My God, it was like she looked into my soul, saw all my fears, my hopes and desires. "See the visions in your mind's eye. Do what you feel in your heart." She was shipping out on this great adventure and she held out her hand to me and said, "Come aboard—let's fight giants together."

> *The song ends. Stage lights off.*

SCENE TWELVE: SHE KISSED ME

The band starts to pack up. One player noodles around on the guitar, underscoring the scene. After a moment, ROSE returns and CLAY points out STUART. ROSE crosses to STUART who stands and pulls out a small,

> *elegant crystal vial and crosses to her. At first he can't speak. Again, as their eyes meet, there is a "ding."*

ROSE   Hi. Adam said you came from all the way from down home.

STUART   Yeah. David Stuart.

ROSE   Hi David.

STUART   Yeah. David and Goliath, right?

ROSE   Right.

STUART   *(He holds out the bottle.)* I was going to Fed Ex this, but decided hand delivery was in order. Salt water.

ROSE   Salt water?

STUART   Right out of Rose Bay. On the South Shore? Dipped it myself last night.

> *She takes the bottle.*

ROSE   *(pause)* Right. Salt water. Wow.

STUART   Your wish is my command.

ROSE   I guess I did ask—in a way.

STUART   In a special kind of way, you know? Music.

ROSE   Yes, very special to me.

STUART   You know, the thing about David is he did more than fight Goliath. He wrote *The Song of Songs*.

ROSE   A songwriter. Guess we have something in common.

STUART   I used to know the whole thing. "Rise up, my love, my fair one, and come away. For, lo, the winter is past, the rain is over and gone."

ROSE   That's beautiful.

STUART   "Many waters cannot quench love, neither can the floods drown it." That's my favourite line.

> *CLAY enters with a digital camera.*

CLAY   Hey you two, how about a shot?

STUART   Really?

CLAY   Hey man, all the way from Nova Scotia. Hey, what's that?

ROSE   Salt water.

CLAY   We're going to put you on the website. Hold it up. Yeah, that's it. *(takes photo)* Got it.

> *CLAY gives the camera to ROSE, then begins to exit. ROSE shows the picture to STUART.*

ROSE   Hey, we look good together.

CLAY   Rose! Let's get goin'.

ROSE   Gotta go. Thanks.

> *She gives him a kiss on the cheek. It's a magical moment. ROSE is gone, leaving STUART touching his cheek in amazement. Underscoring out. Lighting shifts.*

SCENE THIRTEEN: HE DOESN'T HAVE THE HEART TO SEE IN COLOUR

> *In the courtroom STUART stares off into space.*

JUDGE   Mr. Stuart?

> *STUART snaps back into focus.*

STUART   Your Honour, I would just like to point out that Miss Small has admitted she opened a locked door to take my letter. No one in Rose's office has ever refused my letters or indicated by their behaviour they were afraid of me. To my way of thinking, this amounts to an implicit encouragement of my actions.

JUDGE   Very well. Thank you, Miss Small. Next witness.

CROWN   Sergeant Jones, please.

CLERK   Sergeant William Jones, please.

> *JONES enters.*

Hi Bill.

JONES   Hi Len.

JONES is sworn in.

STUART   Jones is one of those fellas who automatically assumes that anyone who falls in love with a star must be an idiot. 'Course, the only thing he's in love with is his uniform.

JONES takes the stand.

CROWN   Sergeant Jones, you are the officer in charge of the Stuart investigation?

JONES   I am, sir.

STUART   Everything is black and white for Jones because he doesn't have the heart to see in colour.

CROWN   And on April 23, 2006 you were assigned to go to Pearson International Airport to pick him up. Is that correct?

JONES   Ah... with the Court's permission, I'd like to refer to my notebook... for the exact times.

JUDGE   When did you make these notes?

JONES   During my investigation of Mr. Stuart.

JUDGE   Have you changed them since?

JONES   Of course not. I just scribbled them down.

JUDGE   *(to STUART)* Do you have any objection to the witness referring to his notebook?

STUART   No, Your Honour. *(to audience)* At least he'll lie in complete sentences.

JUDGE   Very well, you may use your notes to refresh your memory.

JONES   Thank you, Your Honour. *(reads quickly)* "My partner and I arrived at Pearson International Airport at 5:02 p.m. Parked on the arrivals level, Terminal One. We found the accused adjacent to the WestJet ticket counter. Suspect was very angry when we approached him. He said, "I didn't know if—"

JUDGE   Excuse me, Sergeant Jones. I said use the notes to refresh your memory. Do not give a recitation from your notes. You're testifying, not reading us a novel.

JONES   Yes, Your Honour.

CROWN   And is the man you arrested in court today?

JONES   *(points to Stuart)* Yes. That's him.

CROWN   That is the substance of my case, Your Honour. Mr. Stuart presented his letter to Miss Small at the Saltwater office. Miss Small took it and telephoned the police. The call was answered by Sergeant Jones. As Mr. Stuart was in breach of probation, the officer went to the airport and arrested him. He has now identified Mr. Stuart in court today.

JUDGE   You have no further questions?

CROWN   No, Your Honour. I've made my case.

       JONES stands to leave.

JUDGE   Stay.

SCENE FOURTEEN: I CALL IT HARASSMENT

JUDGE   Mr. Stuart?

STUART   Sergeant Jones, do you recall the first arrest you made in regard to this matter of my attention towards Rose McKay?

JONES   *(checks notes)* April 16, 2002. Yes, I have it here in my notes.

STUART   What was the charge?

JONES   Intimidation.

STUART   Who was I supposed to have intimidated?

JONES   Rose McKay.

STUART   And what did Ms. McKay say when she was questioned?

JONES   You know I had no opportunity to question her personally.

STUART   So, I was charged with a serious crime on the basis of hearsay evidence? Is that standard police procedure?

CROWN Your Honour, I can't see what this line of questioning has to do with the case at hand.

STUART Your Honour, I wish to petition the Court during summation that, in fact, my probation is based on a biased and incompetent police investigation.

CROWN Your Honour, this is an absurd charge.

JUDGE Perhaps, but it *is* an interesting defence.

STUART Thank you, Your Honour. You know, one thing binds these two fellas together is their love of paper. They got their notebooks and their transcripts scattered willy-nilly all over my life and a fine hodgepodge they've made of it. I can supply a record of "paperwork errors" going back to my earliest arrest that create an obvious pattern of harassment but—

CROWN Your Honour, there has been no harassment of Mr. Stuart.

STUART Let me just lay out the facts here and let the judge decide. Last spring, after my arrest on the current charges, I got bail so I could go home and open for the tourist season. The Crown then appealed my release, knowing I would be in Nova Scotia and unable to defend myself. I don't know what kind of story Broilman and Jones cooked up but my bail was thereafter revoked.

CROWN What I demonstrated during the appeal was that because of Mr. Stuart's ongoing history of violations an error had been made in releasing him and as a result a warrant was issued for his re-arrest!

STUART Right, a warrant with a phony charge penciled in.

JUDGE A what?

STUART The warrant that I was arrested on said I was wanted on an indictable offence. The charge against me was a summary conviction.

CROWN Your Honour, I don't see how the charge on the warrant, even if it was mistaken, could possibly—

STUART   Sergeant Jones can clarify the advantage of sending out a warrant on an indictable offence can't you, Sergeant Jones?

JONES   There's no advantage.

STUART   Oh come on, Jones. The RCMP get a warrant to pick up an indicted criminal and they take it very seriously and they move on it. But picking up a guy wanted on a miserable little summary offence? No big rush.

JONES   Are you saying I faked that warrant so—

STUART   I'm saying that the RCMP came out on my dock with two hundred people watching me laying the keel on a new dory. You know what an adze is?

JONES   No.

STUART   It's a specialized sideways axe for shaping timbers. Those cops took one look at me swinging it and before I knew it they were all doing the musical ride up and down my backside! Dragged off my own dock in handcuffs, for God's sake!

You know how hard it is to get buses to stop in the middle of nowhere to watch a man build a dory! None of the tour operators sent those buses my way are ever coming back. It took me years to make those contacts and now they are gone. For good. *(beat)* You and Broilman couldn't let me prepare for my trial in peace. No, you had to have me re-arrested so I wouldn't bother a woman living two thousand miles away!

JONES   We had nothing to do with—

STUART   I just proved you did! When I look at the way I've been treated, only one word comes to mind: harassment. I call it harassment.

JONES   And I call it getting a dangerous nutcase off the streets.

STUART   What was that?

JONES   We all remember John Lennon.

STUART   John Lennon! Your Honour!

JUDGE   Sergeant Jones, are you admitting that a warrant was purposely falsified?

JONES   Well...

CROWN   Of course he isn't! Your Honour, while Sergeant Jones perhaps overstates his case, I feel that we must all understand his natural worry over the safety of a star of Ms. McKay's stature—

STUART   There you have it, Your Honour: the Crown is so in awe of Rose's fame that it prejudices my case, and that is a fundamental violation of the principles of justice.

CROWN   Should Rose McKay not have access to the protection of the courts simply because she is famous? Would that be Mr. Stuart's version of justice?

STUART   You don't care about justice, Broilman. All you're concerned about is the prominent place this case has in the public eye.

JUDGE   Now Mr. Stuart...

STUART   The fact is that my conviction, or better yet my committal, will boost his public image!

CROWN   Your Honour, I have had just about enough of Mr. Stuart's slanderous—

JUDGE   Oh, that's enough. Both of you take your seats. Are there any more questions for Sergeant Jones?

CROWN   Sergeant Jones, did you have anything to do with the warrant that was made out for the re-arrest of Mr. Stuart?

JONES   No sir, I did not.

JUDGE   Thank you, Sergeant Jones, you may step down. Go. *(JONES exits.)* Well things have certainly warmed up. Mr. Broilman, what have you to say about Mr. Stuart's charges?

CROWN   I think there is only one comment worth making under the circumstances, Your Honour. Mr. Stuart is deluded.

STUART Your Honour. Mr. Broilman assumes I am deluded about Rose McKay but as I have pointed out again and again, Rose McKay has never been questioned. Since he's never spoken to her and it's an established fact that I have done so on many occasions, it might be more logical to assert that he is delusional.

CROWN Your Honour, I have spoken to Ms. McKay's husband many times. He is eloquent in his description of the problems Mr. Stuart's delusion has created over the last few years. He would be happy to testify.

STUART I object!

SCENE FIFTEEN: ADAM ROCKED MY WORLD

Light shift. During STUART's speech, the band enters playing the intro to "Adam's Rib." They are all dressed like security personnel at a rock concert. This is a highly produced and choreographed number.

STUART Adam Clay. I ask for the queen and they send me her coachman. I mean, we all knew the story—big-time producer on a Cape Breton fishing trip stumbles into a local ceilidh and discovers a girl who sings like an angel. But when the papers announced that they'd been married? I felt like I'd been keelhauled. How could it be possible? For five years I'd been following Rose's every move. I'd kept in touch, and so had she. And then, from out of the blue—nobody really believed they could be in love. He was old enough to be her father. It didn't make sense. I was lost. I had to talk to her. She… she was playing in Toronto. A four-night stand at Massey Hall… so I took another plane.

ROSE sings "Adam's Rib." STUART tries to approach her to give her a rose.

ROSE *Once upon a time I was just a little bone*
I was just a little tiny rib and the rib cage was my home
Some days I'd wonder how it would feel
To be my own person to eat my own meals

Erin McGrath in Western Canada Theatre's and Alberta Theatre Projects' premiere
production of *Still Desire You*. Photo by Murray Mitchell.

I never had to make a plan
Just be a little piece of a bigger man

And Adam rocked my world
I was his biggest fan

No such thing as being a girl
He had the whole world in his hands

Then I started to wonder
What's this spell I might be under
It's time to break away
It's time to feed this hunger

> ROSE kneels in front of STUART and takes the flower.
> Standing right behind her, CLAY takes a guitar break.
> The effect is that he is dominating her and controlling
> her actions. ROSE tosses the flower back to STUART
> and stands, going back into the song.

Never had to take a stand
Just be a little piece of a bigger man
And Adam rocked my world
I was his biggest fan
No such thing as being a girl
He had the whole world in his hands

> STUART jumps onto the stage, trying to get to ROSE,
> but CLAY and the band get between them and STUART
> is dragged offstage.

And Adam rocked my world
I was his biggest fan
No such thing as being a girl
He had the whole world in his hands
The whole wide world in his hands
The whole world in his hands
You and me sister in his hands

> Song ends. ROSE and band exit.

SCENE SIXTEEN: PENMANSHIP

Sound. Rumble of thunder, moderate rainfall, street
noise, horns honking.

STUART turns up his collar and runs across the stage.
We are outside a stage door after the concert. Pre-recorded
underscoring: music from within. STUART stands out-

side the door, program in hand. RICK enters. He's an autograph hunter in a long greasy trench coat.

RICK   Nice weather for July, eh?

STUART   I suppose. *(pause)* Ah... say, this is the stage door, isn't it?

RICK   You kidding? Would I be standing here if it wasn't?

STUART   I don't know.

RICK   No way, man. Rick Phillips doesn't stand around in the deluge unless he can cop some good penmanship, right?

STUART   If you say so...

RICK   Say so, man, I know so. You got any traders?

> *CLAY enters, talking on his cell phone and looking for the limo.*

STUART   Got what?

RICK   Autographs. For swapping.

STUART   I don't collect autographs.

RICK   Then why are you out here in the rain, bub? What are you, a duck?

STUART   I'm waiting to see Rose, she...

SCENE SEVENTEEN: WHAT'S THIS SPELL I'M UNDER

> *ROSE enters. RICK rushes towards her.*

RICK   Ms. McKay! Ms. McKay, could you sign...

CLAY   Sorry, pal. We've got a plane to catch.

> *CLAY gets between RICK and ROSE, moving him away upstage and engaging in a* sotto voce *argument.*

RICK   Aw, come on. All I want is an autograph....

> *ROSE pauses for a second. She seems shaken, looks at STUART, then away as she walks past him.*

STUART   Rose!

ROSE turns and sees him—a "ding."

ROSE Hi, did you see the show?

STUART I wouldn't be here if I hadn't been there.

ROSE All that new material. I was scared to death.

STUART You don't have to be afraid, Rose. I heard what you were saying.

ROSE I wasn't really scared, you know, I just meant...

STUART I heard it. All that overamped BS. You barely got your fiddle out of its case. I know that's not the way you want things to be.

ROSE No, it's great. If you don't grow...

STUART Then why did you sing that song?

ROSE What song?

STUART "What's this spell I might be under. It's time to break away."

ROSE I...

STUART Then him hovering over you like—

Kerfuffle between RICK and CLAY.

RICK It's part of her job.

CLAY That's for me to say, not you.

ROSE Svengali.

STUART Svengali.

ROSE That's what they're calling him—on Much, in papers. Ever since the wedding.... Nothing is ever what it seems and people I counted on just don't understand.

STUART I understand.

ROSE I've never been hated before. And he says, you know, screw 'em. Rub their noses in it and... make it a part of "the act." I don't even remember when it turned into an act.

STUART   Yeah, you're a long way from home.

ROSE   Yeah, I miss the sea.

STUART   It's still there. Fogbound maybe, but it will be there forever. For you.

CLAY crosses to ROSE.

CLAY   There's the limo, sweet thang.

ROSE   Okay.

ROSE takes STUART's program and signs it.

Thanks for coming. It means a lot to me.

ROSE starts to go. STUART grabs her wrist.

STUART   No wait, Rose. Salt water. Rose Bay. Just down the road. We can—

CLAY   Cool your jets, friend.

CLAY takes ROSE's arm away.

ROSE   It's okay, Adam.

STUART   I just wanted to...

CLAY   Get into the limo, Rose. *(pushing STUART away)* You shouldn't grab at people, you know.

ROSE   He didn't mean anything.

STUART   Take your hands off me.

RICK   Hey man, leave the guy alone.

CLAY   Rose! Will you get into the goddamn car?

ROSE exits.

RICK   Ya jerk.

CLAY   Why in the hell can't you treat her like a human being?

CLAY exits.

SCENE EIGHTEEN: I LOVE YOU

RICK   Oh boy, yeah, isn't that typical, eh? Once they start making it big they bring in the goons. Heaven forbid somebody should "touch the star." The dirtbag wouldn't even let me have her autograph. I should have listened to my mother and stayed out of showbiz.

> *STUART ignores all this. He is totally absorbed by ROSE's autograph.*

Say, did you get her?

> *RICK looks over STUART's shoulder and reads.*

Hey, beauty! Give you ten bucks for it.

STUART   What?

RICK   Ten bucks, I'll give you ten bucks. What do you say?

STUART   Don't be ridiculous.

RICK   It's a fair price. I mean, we're not talking about Celine Dion.

STUART   Rose wrote this to me.

RICK   Okay. Okay. I'll trade you. How about... Ben Mulroney? *Canadian Idol.*

STUART   You don't understand. I'm in love with her. I would never part with this program.

RICK   Oh, I got you. You're a Rose McKay freak.

STUART   I'm not a freak. I love her.

RICK   Right, and obviously the feeling is mutual.

STUART   Of course it's mutual. Look, "I love you." That's what she wrote.

RICK   No it's not. What she wrote was I "heart" U. Uuuuuu.

STUART   It's the same thing.

RICK   Yeah, right, except in code. I "heart" you. She's married, dude, and not to you.

STUART   I don't believe it. It's some kind of publicity stunt he cooked up or—she called him Svengali.

RICK   Right, maybe that's code too. Got to be. She really "hearts" U.

STUART   She loves me.

RICK   Why is it every time I come to Massey Hall I end up in conversation with a stalker?

STUART   I'm no stalker!

RICK   Later, lover-boy. See Uuuuuuu.

> *RICK exits, laughing. STUART stares after him. Lights shift.*

SCENE NINETEEN: I AM NOT INSANE!

In the courtroom.

JUDGE   Mr. Stuart?

STUART   What?

JUDGE   Mr. Stuart, do you object to calling Rose McKay's husband to the stand?

STUART   What? Yes, I would object. Clay's testimony is of no more substance than that of Miss Small or any other of Ms. McKay's employees.

CROWN   He is her husband, Your Honour.

STUART   Her alleged husband.

JUDGE   Her alleged husband?

CROWN   This is typical of his thinking, Your Honour. He claims they aren't married.

STUART   That's true. I have reason to believe they are not truly married.

JUDGE   Why do you say they aren't married, Mr. Stuart?

STUART   Your Honour, there are certain personal elements of my relationship with Rose McKay that don't have any place in a court of law.

JUDGE   *(to CROWN)* Do you wish to call Mr. Clay?

STUART   He's a Svengali, a dominating, controlling, lying—

CROWN   Your Honour, why is Mr. Stuart so afraid of confronting Adam Clay on this matter?

STUART   I'm not afraid of him.

CROWN   It's because his whole sick delusion would come crumbling down around him when the Court hears Mr. Clay's testimony about Stuart's visit to Margaree Forks and…

STUART   That son of a bitch would lie about the funeral! He's a big pile of bullshit plopped between Rose and me and I'll be damned if—

JUDGE   Mr. Stuart! Order! I won't tolerate that kind of language in my court!

STUART   Your Honour, it's my life at stake here.

JUDGE   I am aware of that. I have been bending over backwards because you have chosen to proceed without counsel, but there are times when I've felt like you aren't quite with us. I'm afraid I'm going to have to allow Dr. Rand to testify again.

STUART   Your Honour, he's plainly biased in his testimony!

JUDGE   And I will arrange for a second opinion.

STUART   I am not insane!

JUDGE   I don't know if that's true, Mr. Stuart. It's my job to see that if you need help, you get it.

STUART   I'll be happy to have Mr. Clay testify, if that's the matter of concern.

JUDGE   And I'll be happy to hear what he has to say about the… funeral… after we've heard from the doctors. We'll adjourn until Monday. Mr. Broilman, you will arrange for another psychiatrist to talk with Mr. Stuart in the interval.

SCENE TWENTY: HURRICANE

Drumbeat kicks in. Special light on STUART. He packs up his law books and papers, getting ready to return to the hospital.

STUART   After that run-in with Clay everything changed. Rose's career took off like a topping forest fire, and as her fame grew, my access was blocked. Posts to her website, letters, phone calls—taken from me one by one, but at the same time the songs became more personal, more desperate. I didn't know what to do.

> *ROSE appears in a special spotlight; looking exhausted, sitting on a chair wearing headphones, like she's record-ing a song. She's singing "Waiting For The Tide To Turn." STUART begins to cross the stage, leaving the courtroom.*

ROSE   *I cry up to a man in the moon*
He's the only one can help me now

I bought the lie that as long as I tried
I could not leave empty-handed
But I've done all I can do
And now I leave it up to you
I'm waiting for the tide to turn
Waiting for the tide to turn
Waiting, waiting for the tide to take me
To take me away

> *Break. Storm sound effects slowly build.*

STUART   September 28, 2003. Full moon. High tide. Foggy as hell. We all knew the hurricane was coming, but we'd been through big roughs before. I was locked down tight.

ROSE   *Goodnight moon*
I should be talkin' to Neptune
He's the one who will teach me patience

STUART   Bouncing between Rose on Much and the Weather Channel.

ROSE   *For whoever rules the sea*
             Is now the ruler over me

STUART   Then all hell broke lose.

> *A huge crash and flash of lightning. STUART is blasted back to the floor, his books and papers scattered. Guitar solo. The band plays very softly under speech below.*

ROSE   *(under Stuart below) I'm waiting for the tide to turn*
             Waiting for the tide to turn
             Waiting, waiting for the tide to take me
             I'm waiting for the tide to turn
             Waiting for the tide to turn
             Waiting, waiting for the tide to take me

STUART   She came in from the east. Waves seven metres high. The storm surge—higher than the highest tide—lifted the wharf and the gale blasted it to pieces. Railway ties snapped like Popsicle sticks. The dory, mounted on the end of the dock, rose up and came right through that big, plate glass window. Like the wrath of God smashing me in the face. The TV, I swear to God, the TV kept on playing! Her singing that song. With the waves smashing the place to pieces, I grabbed onto the dory and hung on till something hit me hard and that's all I remember.

> *STUART sprawls on the floor.*

ROSE   *So I have proved some things can't be moved*
             And here I wait but my faith is weak,
             And the water's creeping up to my chin
             I'm waiting for the tide to turn
             Waiting for the tide to turn
             Waiting, waiting for the tide to take me
             To take me away

> *The song ends. Studio lighting effects fade out.*

STUART   *(sits up and picks up all his books and papers)* I came to, lying in my dory floating around the shop. Morning was coming, grey, hard, cold. Next thing I remember I was in my house, other side of the road. I got a fire going and made some tea. There was no power. Nothing. I dug out my crank-up radio, got it going and managed to tune in the CBC.

DON (DJ) Among the eight reported deaths is Doctor Joseph McKay, the father of well-known Maritime performer, Rose McKay.

SCENE TWENTY-ONE: THE FUNERAL

A solid musical wail comes from an offstage chorus, like the drone of a bagpipe.

STUART The words rushed through me like a scream of anguish from halfway round the world. When my father died.... It was like the centre of everything fell out of me. And everyone was polite and, "Sorry for your 'troubles.'" But there was no one, brothers, cousins, friends and neighbours.... The flood of emotions the.... No one.... I was the only one who could help her now.

Bagpipe drone. Lights shift. STUART stands on an upstage riser (hillside overlooking a gravesite). A coffin is wheeled on followed by a mourner. ROSE enters (singing) with CLAY, a priest and another mourner.

ROSE sings "Farewell To Nova Scotia."

ROSE *The sun was setting in the west*
The birds were singing on every tree
All nature seemed inclined for a rest
But still there was no rest for me

So farewell to Nova Scotia, the sea-bound coast
Let your mountains dark and dreary be
For when I am far away on the briny ocean tossed
Will you ever heave a sigh and wish for me

STUART Margaree Forks, Cape Breton. The island had been spared the worst of it. A little graveyard on a hill ablaze in the early autumn. Fog hanging in the hollows. The long black hearse taking Rose's daddy home to be buried where he had been born.

ROSE   *(under) I grieve to leave my native home*
I grieve to leave my comrades all
But my captain calls and I must obey
So it's early in the morning
And I am bound far away

> *ROSE plays a verse on the fiddle.*

STUART   I had been lost in a cold and empty world... her songs lifted me up. And now the tide had turned. I was the only one who could help her now. Her faith was weak, she felt like she was drowning, I know, but with love... I knew I could give her back her soul!

ROSE   *For it's early in the morning I am bound far away*

> *Lights fade to black. End of Act One.*

ACT TWO

SOUND COLLAGE

In the black we hear a pre-recorded sound collage. The a capella humming of "Farewell To Nova Scotia" from the end of Act One mixed with fragments of dialogue.

JUDGE   Charged with

CROWN   Suffers from

JUDGE   Did wilfully violate a probation order—

CROWN   An ongoing "infatuation" with singer Rose McKay

ROSE   Send me some salt water

CROWN   Of singing fame

SMALL   Keep in touch

RAND   Erotic paranoia

CROWN   Mentally unfit

JUDGE   Clearly able to defend yourself

RAND   ...test his love

ROSE   What's this spell I might be under

CROWN   Condition must inevitably deteriorate?

RAND   I have no idea what he may do next

ROSE   Waiting for the tide to turn. Waiting for the tide to turn

RICK   Stalker

CROWN   Deluded

ROSE   I love you

CROWN   Adam Clay

ROSE   Svengali

STUART   That son of a bitch would lie

JUDGE   I won't tolerate that kind of language in my court!

STUART   I am not insane!

Clang of door. Lighting effects up.

SCENE TWENTY-TWO: STILL DESIRE YOU

A holding area at the Willows Mental Health Centre. The band plays an ominous riff. Lights up on STUART, who sits on one of six wooden chairs working on a letter. The band and ROSE stand around him. ROSE seems angry, singing directly to him. She scolds and flirts, as if we're watching a stylized version of a couple having a fight.

ROSE
 You leave me wantin' more
 Leave me waiting at the door
 You leave a lot to be desired
 You leave a lot of things unsaid
 Sometimes I say them in my head
 You leave a lot to be desired

 You never make me eggs in the morning
 We never do it on the floor
 You never tell me how good I'm looking
 You don't bring me flowers anymore

 You leave a lot to be desired
 But I still desire you
 And no matter what you do
 I will still desire you

   Break.

 So you won't ever be a star
 So you don't drive a real cool car
 Sometimes it seems like we're at war
 Then I want you even more

 You leave a lot to be desired
 But I still desire you
 And no matter what you do
 I will still desire you

   The band exits still playing. ROSE walks away from STUART, stops, and glares back at him.

You.

>ROSE *exits.*

STUART *(to audience)* Well, here I sit in the holding room at the Willows waiting to try and convince a total stranger that there really is something going on between Rose and I. God, what kind of chance do I have? Any sane man would say I'm crazy. But... I can't get her out of my mind. I know that somehow I've failed her but I just don't know how. I leave a lot to be desired, no doubt about it, but.... My only hope is this trial will once and for all prove my love. Forever.

SCENE TWENTY-THREE: I'M JUST LIKE YOU

GINO *(off)* Take your stinking hands off me, you doorknob's arsehole!

COP *(off)* Will you keep it down?

GINO *(off)* Not much to get it up for in the Willows, is there, Chumley?

COP *(off)* That's your problem, not mine.

>A COP enters with GINO in handcuffs. The COP removes the cuffs.

GINO I am not crazy!

COP The court says you've got a few issues. I think it's called "a flawed belief system."

GINO You're a brain-dead robot. You don't believe in anything!

COP You're in here and I'm not. That says something. *(exits)*

GINO Jesus-Jesus, you monkey-headed bastard! *(to STUART)* Well, what are you looking at?

>STUART looks away.

Oh, sorry to disturb your meditation, man. Just ignore me. That shrink just stuck my johnson in a light socket and flipped the switch, but what's it mean to you, right?

STUART   Who was it?

GINO   Eh?

STUART   What was the psychiatrist's name?

GINO   C.G. Rand. What's it to you anyway? Say, wait a minute. I know you. Dave Stuart, right? Wow. I don't believe it, I've seen your picture in the paper. Man, like, you're a folk hero, right?

STUART   What are you talking about?

GINO   Rose McKay, man. That's huntin' for bear. You really love her, right? *(pause)* Hey, what's the matter? You deaf? You love Rose McKay, right?

STUART   I'm in here because of her. You might say the romance is at a low ebb.

GINO   Well don't say she didn't warn you.

STUART   What do you mean?

GINO   That song—"The Mermaid."

> *GINO sings "The Mermaid of Port Mouton."*

> *And though I could not swim, I jumped right in*
> *And sank beneath the salty swell*

> *GINO laughs loudly, then becomes deadly serious.*

See, what worries me is how do you know for sure? I mean, you can think somebody loves you, give up everything for them but how do you know for sure? How can you ever really know if someone loves you?

STUART   That, my friend, is a huge question.

GINO   I'm working at this Lexus dealership in Windsor, right, detailing cars, which is my thing, and the guy who owns the place has this daughter, right? And she is something else. Seventeen. Hair down to here. She's always wearing this black leotard thing from her yoga class, right? First day I see her, she walks by, "Hi Gino!" *(pause)* I watch her pass… and the future opens up… and I see how it is going to be. Me and Cathy. Meant. To. Be. But wait, B.S.P.

Big Social Problem. Who was I to be messin' with the boss's daughter, right? I mean, this guy's worth millions and there's his precious little yoga princess and there's me... a car fluffer with bad skin and a wop name. But none of that mattered 'cause Cathy and me, right from the get-go, we connect. Bang. Electricity. One day her old man caught us together, I'm standing close, right, holding her hand. The bastard goes berserk and fires me on the spot.

(pause) But by then I knew the whole pattern. I followed her to school. Hung out at the coffee shop down the street, detailing the plan. We were in love. Nothing else mattered. I kept chipping away until Cathy gave me her cell number. Key to the highway, right? Call her after midnight and whisper in her ear. Chip, chip, chipping away.

Then came the day. I appropriate the best Lexus on her daddy's lot. A big black SC430 retractable hardtop coupe! And we took off. Gino and Cathy peel away into the night!

STUART She loved you?

GINO It was heaven, man. It was going to be perfect.

STUART Well... what... what happened?

GINO I'm asleep in the back of the car. Wake up beside this fly-speckled garage on the side of the road in Nevada. Cathy's gone. I find her inside the diner. She's on the phone to her goddamn father! Women, man. They light the fuse, they pay the price. I hit her. Just once. Open palm. Okay, more than once but open palm, see... oh God, I hit her too hard... I... blood... cops. *(pause)* I'm not crazy. I did it for love, you know, like you, you know?

STUART You are nothing like me! You... you hurt that girl... you can't... you never, ever hurt someone you love.

GINO She hurt me worse! What do you know? Were you there?

STUART No!

GINO   Were you there!

> *GINO knocks over three chairs and goes after STUART, who tries to defend himself, but he's not a fighter. He tries to back away but one quick punch knocks him down.*

That bitch… she says she loves me and the next minute she's calling her old man, the rotten little…. You're just like me and you know it!

> *GINO kicks STUART in the stomach. The COP rushes back into the room and puts GINO in a chokehold.*

COP   Stop it right now you creep or I'll put you out.

> *GINO stops struggling.*

You okay?

STUART   Get that pathetic little animal out of here!

> *The COP drags GINO away.*

GINO   Pathetic? I'm just like you, Stuart! And you know it! Just like you! Just like you!

> *GINO exits. STUART lies on the floor gasping for breath.*

SCENE TWENTY-FOUR: HEALING ANGEL

> *ROSE enters and kneels beside STUART. She sings "I Can't Take My Eyes Off You."*

ROSE   *So dear to me*
Always keep me company
No need to go outside
I will be your silent bride
I can't take my eyes off you

> *STUART slowly begins to pull himself together and sits up. He rights a chair, straightens up the waiting room. ROSE stands and watches him.*

Nothing ever needs to be said
You send your message

> Right into my head
> You fill me up when I'm alone
> So soothing is your monotone

    ROSE is close. They look at each other intently.

I can't take my eyes off you

ROSE & STUART   *I can't take my eyes off you*

ROSE   *I can't take my eyes off you*

ROSE & STUART   *I can't take my eyes off you*

    They dance together—but still apart.

ROSE   Do do do do doooooh
    Do do do do do dooooh
    Do do do dooh

    So maybe you're not as real as the others
    But I choose you over all my past lovers
    For they have come and they have gone
    But I can always turn you on

    I can't take my eyes off you

ROSE & STUART   *I can't take my eyes off you*

ROSE   *I can't take my eyes off you*

ROSE & STUART   *I can't take my eyes off you*

    ROSE approaches STUART. Once more they almost touch but as the song ends she exits. He stands looking after her.

SCENE TWENTY-FIVE: DO YOU BELIEVE IN LOVE?

    STUART doesn't notice as DOWNEY enters.

DOWNEY   Mr. Stuart, I'm Kim Downey. The shrink the court wants you to talk to. Call me Kim, okay?

    STUART doesn't respond.

I know you must be frightened but I'm on your side.
(pause) All I want to do is help you. *(pause)* Mr. Stuart, are
you okay?

STUART   I don't know…

DOWNEY   What's the matter? *(pause)* Look, Mr. Stuart, I can't help
you if you won't talk to me.

STUART   David?

DOWNEY   Pardon?

STUART   My name is David.

DOWNEY   Okay, David. Listen, we don't have a whole lot of time. If
you want me to help you get out of this jam, then you've
got to help me. I've been looking through your file and I
don't think what they've done to you is fair. I mean… Dr.
Rand has certainly put together a neat little package here.
(her files) I've never seen such a pack of half-baked
assumptions in my life.

STUART   You don't think I'm…?

DOWNEY   The last time you were committed you behaved pretty
sensibly. You sold the board of review, that's for sure.
(pause) In fact David, I think you must be a pretty stable
guy to keep your head together in this zoo.

STUART   No iatrogenesis.

DOWNEY   Iatrogenesis?

STUART   An illness arising during the treatment of another malady.
Being in the Willows can drive you crazy.

DOWNEY   Right. That's pretty high-flown talk for a carpenter from
Nova Scotia.

STUART   I've been in here often enough to have done my research.
I don't think I can take another stretch. My every waking
moment's spent in the company of sick, dangerous men.

DOWNEY   Yeah, and then there are the patients.

> They laugh together.

We've only got one real problem in this case, David.

STUART   What's that?

DOWNEY   You claim you and Rose McKay are in love. It's pretty hard to argue a guy's total sanity when he's making a claim like that.

STUART   Why is that so darn hard to believe?

DOWNEY   (checks her files) Well, according to Rand you believe she sends you secret messages.

STUART   We find ways to communicate. Look at it this way, Doctor, I become an admirer of Rose McKay's and I join her fan club. Make regular visits to her website. You use the web, right?

DOWNEY   Sure.

STUART   You know about cookies?

DOWNEY   Not really.

STUART   Little programs that download to your computer from websites. You don't even know. Some are useful, some... spyware, adware. I mean, I have a tracker on the FOG Shop site tells me more about my prospective customers than you can imagine. It would take nothing for Rose to know that I stream her videos from her site—all the rest.

DOWNEY   So the secret messages are in her songs.

STUART   Not exactly.... I know how it sounds, but God, you hear stranger things on the news every night!

DOWNEY   Yeah, but the newscaster isn't facing a fitness hearing that could put him in the Willows.

STUART   Do you believe in love?

DOWNEY   Sometimes.

STUART   Do you remember what it's like the first time? Thinking about the other person all day long. And maybe there's a song... your song, and every time you turn on the radio they seem to be playing it... and you know how sometimes you just pick up the phone on a whim and call and that other person says... "I was just thinking about you."

STILL DESIRE YOU • 59

DOWNEY smiles.

You know what I'm talking about.

DOWNEY Yeah, I've been in love.

DOWNEY laughs.

STUART When those little magic moments come along you don't question your sanity. You just sit back and think… "that's so beautiful."

DOWNEY Damn, David, the synchronicity of love isn't going to carry your case in court. People just won't buy it.

STUART That's because we live in a world that feeds on loneliness and fear, not love. Every time you turn on a TV you just get pounded. Death, destruction. Suicide bombers. Kids gunned down on Main Street. You hardly know your neighbours. You live in a city a thousand miles away from the place you were born and the people you love. There's no contact. There's nothing real.

DOWNEY Everything you say may be true but it's not going to help me in court. If you'd just go in there and admit you made a mistake—

STUART I can't do that. I mean, I loved my father, you know? Saw him every day, just about. Lived with him, worked with him. Nursed him two full years when he was on his way out. Most people thought I was crazy then, too. Why? Because I wouldn't lock him up in "a nice facility" like "normal people" do. No sir. That's no way to live. You love somebody, you do it for keeps. So I will never deny my love for Rose until the day I hear her deny her love for me. I don't believe that's going to happen. And as my old man used to say, "That's the it of it."

DOWNEY What's your final outcome?

STUART What do you mean?

DOWNEY How do you think this relationship will work out in the end?

STUART   Best-case scenario? Rose comes to court. I'm acquitted. She retires, we get married, live in Blue Rocks, raise a family. Maybe she opens a tea house next to the shop. Hey, it worked for Rita. Anybody with a dream like that should be committed, eh?

DOWNEY   Well... I guess I'll have to concentrate on convincing them you just aren't "mean" enough to be locked up. See you in court. *(exits)*

STUART   *(to audience)* It is my certain belief that love can, and will, save the world. And if that is true I can win this thing and then.... Best-case scenario? A kitchen party.

> As he speaks all the members of the court enter carrying instruments.

SCENE TWENTY-SIX: HAPPY HOMEMAKERS

ALL   *(offstage)* Hi Dave!

> A kitchen party breaks out. Members of the court play an instrumental version of "The Mermaid of Port Mouton."

JUDGE   Now this is more like it.

CROWN   Summer down here's the only thing keeps me sane.

RAND   *(to STUART)* By the way, you were right, I was wrong. You're not crazy. Sorry about that.

> As the music ends.

DOWNEY   *(a toast)* Sociable!

STUART   What should we play now?

> All at once.

JUDGE   "St. Anne's Reel"

CROWN   "Aunt Martha's Sheep"!

DOWNEY   "The Mira."

CLERK   "Rise Again"!

RAND   "Headin' for Halifax."

DOWNEY   "Snowbird."

ALL   No!

> *ROSE enters.*

JUDGE   Order! Order in the court.

ROSE   Let's do "Happy Homemaker"!

> *Maybe I'd be happy to let it all go*
> *Dedicate my life to making jelly moulds*
> *Learn to cook and learn to sew. Ahhhh—*

STUART & ROSE   *A happy homemaker*

ROSE   *Why have I been pushing so hard*
When I could be out in the backyard
Letting down my hair
Letting down my guard

ALL   *Ahhhhh...*

ROSE   *Happy homemaker*
Barefoot and pregnant never looked so good
We're all dying to take our shoes off
Never what we want it's always what we should

ALL   *Ahhh, Ahhh, Ahhh, Ahhh,*

ROSE   *A happy homemaker*
I know it'll be different this time 'round

STUART   *We'll put to use the wisdom I hope we've found*

ROSE   *Like to lose the crap without losing ground*
I'm a happy homemaker

BOTH   *Barefoot and pregnant never looked so good*

ALL   *We're all dying to take our shoes off*

ROSE   *Gone so far the other way*
We're scared to be our mothers
And we're scared of going soft

> *Musical break. Cast clogs during the chorus.*

BOTH   *Barefoot and pregnant*
Never looked so good

ALL   *We're all dying to take our shoes off*
Never what we want
It's always what we should

Ahhh, Ahhh, Ahhh, Ahhh, Ahhh

ROSE   *A happy homemaker*

        The song ends.

        ROSE takes a fiddle break as chairs are cleared and the
        courtroom is re-established.

SCENE TWENTY-SEVEN: MR. STUART'S CONDITION WILL DETERIORATE

    Fantasy and reality are overlapping even in court. ROSE
    hovers upstage watching the proceedings. The CLERK
    underscores the action with hints of "Waiting For The
    Tide." DR. RAND sits in the witness box.

STUART   Okay. Bring 'er on.

CROWN   Dr. Rand, would it be fair to say Mr. Stuart may be suffering from schizophrenia?

RAND   The existence of paranoia without the presence of schizophrenia is quite rare. In the case of an encapsulated delusional system like Mr. Stuart's, the patient may at first only suffer from the delusion itself, but usually a schizophrenic element develops. Given similar cases, one would expect Mr. Stuart's condition to deteriorate.

    Yes.

CROWN   Why is that?

RAND   He is involved in very stressful situations; prison, the failure of his business...

STUART   *(to audience)* Or to put it another way, "We're driving him crazy."

CROWN   And what would be the result of this... deterioration?

RAND   Well, almost anything could happen. He could become unpredictable, perhaps violent.

STUART   Notice it took him two "coulds," an "unpredictable" and one "perhaps" to get to violent. That's a sizable number of hops across the ice floe, isn't it?

CROWN   Your experience with Mr. Stuart does lead you to believe he is deteriorating?

RAND   Yes. The delusional system seems to have expanded to include the court, and his illness has clearly come to encompass our attempts at treatment.

STUART   Your Honour. I object.

JUDGE   Yes?

STUART   I think I pretty much established the other day that there's been a pattern of harassment in the actions of both the Crown and Dr. Rand and now we're back to calling the facts I'm presenting here a delusion.

JUDGE   You'll have your chance, Mr. Stuart.

CROWN   Dr. Rand, do you feel that Mr. Stuart is fit to stand trial?

RAND   No sir, I do not.

CROWN   Thank you. Nothing further, Your Honour.

JUDGE   Mr. Stuart?

>   *STUART stands, preparing to speak. Underscoring shifts. The CLERK on guitar plays "Waiting For The Tide To Turn." ROSE sings in a whisper.*

ROSE   *(sings) Waiting for the tide to turn. Waiting for the tide to turn.*

STUART   Thank you, Your Honour. Clearly Dr. Rand's testimony about the "deterioration" of my "condition" is speculative at best and at heart rests on a wilful avoidance of the facts. Dr. Downey is going to be called in this matter?

JUDGE   Yes, she is.

STUART   In that case I have no further questions for Dr. Rand. I would prefer to have my mental state assessed by a more impartial authority.

JUDGE   You may step down, Dr. Rand.

ROSE   (sings) Waiting, waiting, waiting for the tide to take me away.

SCENE TWENTY-EIGHT: WHERE HE WOULD RECEIVE TREATMENT

> RAND exits as DR. DOWNEY enters, takes the stand
> and is sworn in.

ROSE   I cry up to a man in the moon
            He's the only one can help me now
            I bought the line that as long as I tried
            I could not leave empty-handed
            But I've done all I can do
            And now I leave it up to you

            And I'm waiting for the tide to turn
            Waiting for the tide...

CROWN   Dr. Downey, have you had a chance to speak with the accused?

DOWNEY Yes, I have.

CROWN   Would you concur with Dr. Rand's opinion that Mr. Stuart is unfit to stand trial?

DOWNEY I don't believe that's even the issue.

CROWN   Dr. Rand is adamant, in his opinion Mr. Stuart is slipping into a schizophrenic state.

DOWNEY I saw no evidence of that.

STUART (to audience) This girl's a dream come true.

CROWN   Are you saying there is no chance he is a danger to himself or other persons in the community?

DOWNEY This is a very complex issue. The best predicator of future dangerousness is past dangerousness. Mr. Stuart appears to be a very gentle man and there is no evidence of violent behaviour in the past.

CROWN   But Dr. Rand has indicated that if... if delusions expand beyond their encapsulated form, schizophrenic behaviour will begin to occur. I take it we agree that Mr. Stuart's delusional system is expanding?

DOWNEY I don't think so.

CROWN But his delusion now encompasses the actions of the police and the proceedings of this court.

DOWNEY To put it bluntly, I don't think it's particularly insane for Mr. Stuart to feel he has been victimized by this system.

CROWN Victimized?

DOWNEY It is reprehensible that someone like Mr. Stuart faces incarceration in an institution for the criminally insane.

CROWN I wonder if you'd feel the same way if you were being bothered by Mr. Stuart. Is it not fair to say that you would feel personally violated?

STUART *(stands)* Your Honour—"violated!"

> *DOWNEY gestures for him to sit down, she'll handle it. STUART sits, looks at ROSE.*

ROSE *(sings)* ...*Teach me patience*...

DOWNEY "Violated"—that's a loaded term, isn't it?

CROWN It makes the point.

DOWNEY I suppose it does—the point being that we're a society drunk on fear that seems incapable of differentiating between an occasional, irritating intrusion and "violation."

CROWN You believe *that* is the issue?

DOWNEY I believe that people should be punished for what they do, not what they think.

CROWN Your Honour, the question at hand is whether Mr. Stuart is dangerous.

ROSE *(sings, under)* Waiting, waiting...

DOWNEY A more pertinent question is, "How long will we continue to allow our system to feed victims into institutions just because we have no other place to put them?"

JUDGE The question before this court is neither of the above. I want to know if this man is able to defend himself.

DOWNEY Your Honour, sending this man to the Willows on a Lieutenant Governor's warrant is, in my opinion, the worst thing that could happen to him.

JUDGE Dr. Downey, this courtroom is not a forum for your social views. You will confine yourself to answering the Crown's questions.

DOWNEY But, Your Honour—

JUDGE Do you have any doubts about Mr. Stuart's ability to stand trial?

DOWNEY Psychiatry is not a precise science. There are always doubts, but...

CROWN Can you categorically deny the possibility that Mr. Stuart may, in the future, deteriorate into a violent schizophrenic state?

DOWNEY Not categorically but... Mr. Stuart's essentially harmless delusion may be classified as a mental illness but—

> *Music out. ROSE stands, watching. At an appropriate point in the action she'll slip off, unnoticed by STUART.*

STUART *(stands)* No, that's not right!

JUDGE Sit down, Mr. Stuart.

CROWN What might push him over the edge?

DOWNEY As Dr. Rand suggests, stress, but—

CROWN The stress of repeated court appearances?

DOWNEY Perhaps.

CROWN The stress of seeing his business fail after he misses the tourist season?

DOWNEY Well maybe, but...

CROWN And above all, the stress of his continued rejection by Rose McKay?

DOWNEY No, above all, the stress of being locked up in a hospital for the criminally insane.

CROWN   Where he would receive treatment. No further questions, Your Honour.

JUDGE   Do you have any questions for Dr. Downey?

STUART   I certainly do. Dr. Downey, on what do you base your belief that I am deluded?

DOWNEY   On the basis of our interview at the Willows.

STUART   But you said you understood.

DOWNEY   I understand why you feel like you do, David, but it's not real. Eventually you'll see that.

STUART   You told me you were "the psychiatrist for the defence."

DOWNEY   I'm trying to help you get the right kind of treatment.

STUART   I don't need help. I need... *(to JUDGE)* Your Honour, there seems that based upon... there seems to be some indication that you may find my arguments before this court irrelevant to my case. Before you take that position, I would just like to point out one more time that there has been no real attempt to discover the true facts behind my case. Rose McKay—

> *STUART turns to look at ROSE. She's gone.*

Rose McKay has never been questioned.

JUDGE   Mr. Stuart, if you'll recall there was an attempt to look into your allegations. Mr. Clay is willing to testify to your behaviour. Upon this suggestion you became irrational in your objections.

STUART   Rose is the only one who can explain what's going on.

JUDGE   The Crown claims Mr. Clay can be of assistance.

STUART   Look, Your Honour, if it will prevent you from ruling against me, I'll talk to the man, but it won't solve anything.

JUDGE   Call Adam Clay.

CLERK   Adam Clay!

JUDGE   Thank you, Leonard.

SCENE TWENTY-NINE: THE FUNERAL AGAIN

*Music underscore: "Farewell To Nova Scotia" hummed
by cast in a drone. Lights shift. We leave the courtroom
and go again to the fantasy sequence funeral. SANDY,
a workman, enters. STUART observes the action from
a distance. SANDY sneaks a drink—STUART notices.
SANDY notices him. Live sound: drumbeats.*

SANDY Cold enough to freeze the best bits off a brass monkey, ain't she?

STUART Do you think drinking is appropriate today?

SANDY Nobody up here but you. *(pause)* It's just that I can't stand funerals. Scare me to death the way everything suddenly gets so permanent.

STUART Well, if you don't like it, why did you come?

SANDY I dig the holes.

STUART Oh.

SANDY *(intake of breath on "yups")* Yup, yup, yup. I mean, it's steady work, right? I can't be complaining... but I just don't understand why people put themselves through all this malarkey. I mean, it doesn't do the guy in the box any good now, does it?

STUART The funeral isn't for the deceased. It's a time for the living to gather strength from each other.

SANDY You sound like a funeral director.

STUART I hate funerals. But it will help Rose.

SANDY She a friend of yours?

STUART Look at her down there. Like a little bird brought to ground.

SANDY You from T.O.? You work with Rose or something? *(no answer)* Hey, buddy!

STUART Why don't you just watch the funeral?

SANDY You know, if you're such a friend, how come you aren't with the funeral party?

STUART   I'll go to her when the time is right.

SANDY   You're not family. You just some kind of... fan, aren't you? As in fan-a-tic.

STUART   I'm here for Rose. She knows that.

SANDY   Ah, this is ghoulish.

       SANDY exits.

SCENE THIRTY: DEEP DOWN YOU KNOW

CLAY enters and walks up to STUART.

CLAY   David Stuart, right? The love letters in the shaker boxes, the flask of salt water, the airplane ticket... did I get that right?

STUART   It's none of your business who I am.

CLAY   Would you mind telling me what in hell you all are doing here?

STUART   I think I have a right to share in Rose's grief.

CLAY   Look down there. They are putting her father in the ground. You have no right to bring more pain to the table.

STUART   Rose wants me to be here.

CLAY   Rose does not want you here. You are intruding on her grief.

STUART   You know that's not true.

CLAY   Then why did she send me up here to get rid of you?

STUART   You're the one who's out of place here, not me.

CLAY   That so?

STUART   You know nothing about how we do things here. You fill Rose's mind with confusion, pull her away from the things that are real. You can hear it all in her songs.

CLAY   Hear it in her songs? Damn it all, Stuart, this isn't some fantasy world whipped up off the radio! *This is reality!*

Rose's father is dead and you can't do a damn thing to help her. You just hurt her by showin' up.

STUART Don't you think I know how desperate and lonely she is? Can't you hear what she's singing about? No, I guess you're so in love with the sound of cash registers that you can't hear anything else.

CLAY Just pack it in, okay?

STUART I think I'd better talk to Rose.

CLAY Fine. Come on down the hill. Quote her a lyric. You'll get a real good dose of reality when you see what's in her eyes.

STUART With you hovering over the proceedings like a vulture?

CLAY Don't worry. I'll give you all the room you need to ruin her father's funeral.

STUART You just go about your business, Clay, and I'll go about mine.

CLAY You're afraid of her, aren't you? 'Cause way down deep you know she doesn't give a damn about you.

STUART That's a g.d. lie!

CLAY I think you'd better go before I call the police.

STUART You're nothing but a sleazy showbiz hustler sucking Rose's blood and—

CLAY That's it. Move it or I'm going to pop you one. No joke.

STUART Then who'd be ruining the funeral?

CLAY You've already done that, Mr. Stuart. Now move it, because if you don't, things are going to get very messy, very fast. I SAID MOVE IT!

> *Drum beats as lights change. CLAY and STUART move into the courtroom.*

SCENE THIRTY-ONE: THE BREAKDOWN

CLAY   Well, after that business at the funeral… things were getting out of hand on all fronts. The harassment had to stop. So we took the necessary steps. In the last two years we put about three hundred thousand dollars into security systems. And as far as Mr. Stuart goes, well, he'd come to the house, as I've said, so the next time he came to the office we phoned the police. It's beyond me how he can say Rose never discouraged him. If I'd been dragged through the courts the number of times he has, I'd sure feel discouraged. And that's about it.

JUDGE   Very well, Mr. Stuart, do you have any questions?

STUART   Yes, Your Honour. Mr. Clay, you claim my "harassment" of Ms. McKay has led to the installation of expensive security systems. Is it unusual for a performer of Ms. McKay's public stature to be highly security conscious?

CLAY   Sadly, you don't have much choice. Once a career gets to a certain point a performer needs protection from guys like you.

STUART   I see. Then you would have installed security systems regardless of my involvement with Ms. McKay? Now, you testified that I came to the house in Toronto, is that correct?

CLAY   Yeah. And the cottage in Margaree.

STUART   Mr. Clay, isn't it a fact that the real issue here isn't my occasional visit to Rose's home. It was my attendance at her father's funeral that pushed you over the edge.

CLAY   The funeral?

STUART   Of Ms. McKay's father.

CLAY   You weren't at the funeral.

STUART   You just testified that I came to the—

CLAY	I just testified that this other creep showed up at the funeral. That made us decide we had to shut down all the people bothering Rose. You included.
STUART	You claim I didn't come to the funeral?
CLAY	I just told the court. You came to the house. I invited you in to try and reach some understanding about this whole situation. We had words and you left. You didn't show up at the funeral.
STUART	Then... why ... why was I arrested after the funeral?
CLAY	Didn't you hear a word I said? You weren't there.
STUART	It was up on the hill... in the graveyard. We almost came to blows.
CLAY	The graveyard isn't on a hill, not the Catholic one, anyway.
STUART	Why... why would I lie about something like that? It's here... it was even in the paper... here in my... my scrapbook...

> STUART leafs through his scrapbook.

Here... it's "Rose McKay Tops Billboard Chart...." No, "McKay Plays the Pump..." "Triumph at Massey Hall..." "Still a Down Home Girl." No it's "Psychiatrist Claims Ardent Fan Mentally Ill..." no... yes. Yes... here it is! "The Price of Fame." "An unwelcome guest leant a sour note to the funeral of Rose McKay's father in Margaree Forks yesterday. The would-be songwriter approached Ms. McKay during the burial service and—"

CLAY	Mr. Stuart, you aren't a songwriter.

> STUART realizes he's way off base.

STUART	Well, I... I wanted to be at the funeral... I... I knew Rose would need someone to stand by her. But... but... my shop was destroyed. The storm knocked out everything, I... when I thought about the reporters, all the people who wouldn't know me, and what was really going on,

I... I was with her in spirit. *(pause)* I failed Rose, didn't I? That's why she's doing this.

JUDGE   *(pause)* Mr. Stuart, are you all right?

SCENE THIRTY-TWO: THE TRUTH

STUART   Your Honour. I... I realize that I have made a mistake. My... the pressure of the trial has led me to mistake the occasion to which Mr. Clay was referring. He is correct in saying that I... I... Your Honour, this mistake on my part in no way alters the fact that... I have sent or given Rose McKay over a hundred separate items, including a vial of salt water. Salty tears. She has never returned one of them, yet I am to be found insane because... from time immemorial, man has been encouraged to play the role of pursuer in male/female relationships. All the old songs— no, in real life, the fact that I am pursuing a woman is not insane. I have never forced my attentions on Rose. My great crime, remember, is bringing her a love letter. That's all, but because of Rose McKay's fame the court suggests psychiatric imprisonment.

JUDGE   Mr. Stuart, the issue here is not imprisonment, it's treat-ment. If you require psychiatric help—

STUART   The board of review doesn't think I need help.

JUDGE   I'll decide if you need help. You can count on that.

STUART   She's manipulating the proceedings... her spirit hovers over this courtroom. If it didn't, then why are there reporters off in the corner taking such voracious notes?

JUDGE   Mr. Stuart—

STUART   If the court wishes to prove me deluded have Rose McKay come in here and deny what I'm saying. Have Rose McKay come in here and say she is afraid of me, that she feels endangered by me, that she personally does not want me to ever write to her again. Have her return my mail and tell me to go away. Then, if I persist in my behaviour, then your doubts about my mental competence may have some basis in fact and I'll plead guilty. I'll seek help, but until the court takes this step, I am a victim of abuse.

SCENE THIRTY-THREE: AVENGING ANGEL

CLAY Your Honour, if I can interrupt here, we have had enough of Mr. Stuart's implications that somehow Rose is pushing him around. She's taping a show just down the street. I can have her here in five minutes. Let's lay this whole thing to rest once and for all.

JUDGE Ms. McKay agrees to testify?

STUART That's all I'm asking for.

JUDGE Well then, call Rose McKay.

> *Dramatic lighting shift. Music intro begins as ROSE enters. Her costume is extreme—futuristic, a menacing avenging angel. She sings "Bionic."*

ROSE *Now that I'm strong*
Can't remember how I used to be
I'm a virtual Amazon
And there's no way you can get to me

It's the answer I've been looking for
I don't want to be human anymore

I'm bionic
Supersonic
I am superhuman
I am supernatural

Never been so high
Love my six million dollar smile
Look how fast I can run
Never going back to where I come from

It's the answer I've been looking for
I don't want to be human anymore

I'm bionic
Supersonic

Sarah Donald, Erin McGrath and John Murphy in Western Canada Theatre's and Alberta Theatre Projects' premiere production of *Still Desire You*. Photo by Murray Mitchell.

> *I am superhuman*
> *I am supernatural*
>
> *No more being unhappy*
> *No more pain can touch me*
> *We have the technology*
> *Bigger, stronger, faster*
>
> > *Instrumental solo.*
>
> *I'm not what I used to be*
> *No one's got the better of me*
> *It's the answer I've been looking for*
> *I don't want to be human anymore*
>
> *I'm bionic*
> *I'm supersonic*
> *I am superhuman*
> *I am supernatural*
>
> > *The song ends, lights shift. ROSE freezes in the spotlight until band exits. She turns into the court scene.*

SCENE THIRTY-FOUR: SORRY YOU GOT HURT

In the courtroom.

STUART Rose!

JUDGE Would you like to be seated, Ms. McKay?

ROSE Yes, I would. I'm sorry about the way I'm dressed but I was filming.

JUDGE It's quite all right. You look... lovely. Mr. Broilman?

CROWN Thank you, Your Honour. I have only one question for this witness. Did you request that your husband institute legal proceedings against David Stuart?

ROSE Yes, I did.

JUDGE Ms. McKay, why is that?

ROSE Sometimes fans who at first seem harmless... a long time ago Mr. Stuart came to one of my shows and gave me a bottle of salt water—a reference to one of my songs. It was a nice gesture and I wrote him a note thanking him and then he started writing all the time, showing up at concerts and so on, and it just went from there—until he started to come to our summer place and then to our home in Toronto. He seemed to have no regard for the people around me and I became very concerned about what might happen. So I had Adam phone the police to see if they could help keep Mr. Stuart away.

CROWN Nothing more, Your Honour. Ms. McKay's statement supports my case.

JUDGE Mr. Stuart, do you have any questions to ask the witness?

STUART Yes, Your Honour, I do. Do you recall when you appeared in Vancouver at a club called The Town Pump?

ROSE Yes. That's quite a while back.

STUART Do you recall meeting me?

ROSE Not particularly.

STUART   But that was the occasion on which I gave you the salt water. We had our picture taken together.

ROSE   Over time my concerts tend to blur together.

STUART   Still, you remember the event and admit you wrote to me personally, at least on one occasion.

ROSE   I've already said so.

STUART   Can you tell us about the substance of our conversation on that occasion?

ROSE   I don't remember.

STUART   We discussed your song "Goliath." And *The Song of Songs*. Written by the same David who battled Goliath. Do you remember that?

ROSE   Yeah… I think… maybe.

STUART   *(pulling out a clipping)* One reviewer has pointed out that, "You use metaphoric references to many elements of our 'cultural zeitgeist' within your work." Would you agree with that statement?

ROSE   I'm not even sure what it means.

STUART   Neither was I, so I got out the dictionary. That fella could have used smaller words and got the job done quicker. What he meant was that your songs use stories from the Bible, references to cartoon heroes, television programs, like that.

ROSE   I suppose.

STUART   —and also frequent references to our shared Maritime heritage—salt water, the tide and so on?

ROSE   Yes.

STUART   The critic called that your "artistic strategy" but, near as I can tell, you're just doing what all the old songs from down home do as a matter of course. So, it comes natural.

ROSE   I suppose so, in a way.

STUART   The old songs are full of things that don't make much sense when you first look at them, but cut deep, you know? The critic guy calls 'em "penetrating symbolic transfers of information."

ROSE   I'm sorry, I don't—

STUART   For instance, in "Adam's Rib" you make reference to the Bible—but at the same time your alleged husband's name is Adam, which implies an expression of a real struggle for independence in your life.

ROSE   That wasn't my intent.

STUART   Or, likewise the implicit reference to David, my name, in "Goliath"; "I know I've got something inside of me. Just like I know you've got something inside of you."

ROSE   I don't think you understand.

STUART   "I can't take my eyes off you. So dear to me always, keep me company. Who needs to go outside? I will be your silent bride." Don't you see the contradiction in claiming you won't see me and then sending me that kind of symbolic encouragement?

ROSE   Oh for God's sake, that song was dedicated to my TV set!

JUDGE   Mr. Stuart, it is clear that your interpretations of Ms. McKay's "symbolic communications" are incorrect. Can we go on to something more concrete?

STUART   What about the letters, Your Honour? *(to ROSE)* You wrote to me personally on at least one occasion. The salt water letter?

ROSE   Yes.

STUART   Isn't it possible that you wrote more letters which you have now conveniently forgotten?

ROSE   I didn't write any more letters.

STUART   Did you have someone write letters?

ROSE   No.

STUART   Did you dictate letters over the phone?

ROSE   I did not.

STUART   Did you cause letters to be written to me?

ROSE   No.

STUART   Come on, Rose, of course you did. Whose office did the letters come from? Whose publicity machine have I supposedly confused with the real person? Who is responsible for all the encouragement I've received over the years? Who is responsible, Rose? *(pause)* You are responsible.

> *A long pause. ROSE thinks about what's he's said. There is another "ding." Lights shift.*

ROSE   Look, Mr. Stuart.

STUART   David, please. There's no one here but us.

ROSE   Mr. Stuart, I sing songs for a living. They're not symbolic for me. They're just good songs. I—

STUART   Don't be afraid of your feelings, Rose. Just because people in the courtroom don't understand…

ROSE   You're in great danger, Mr. Stuart. Do you understand that? This is not a relationship. It's a legal proceeding in a court of law. That judge has the power to institutionalize you. Maybe for the rest of your life.

STUART   Now don't you worry about that, Rose.

ROSE   How am I supposed to "not worry"? I'm a human being, not a machine. You just said I was responsible for all this trouble you're in.

STUART   I know you were angry, that you felt I failed you, but Rose… I…

ROSE   Listen to me. I am trying to help you. You've got to come back to the real world. Get a lawyer who can help you. They might even let you go.

STUART   They have to let me go, Rose.

ROSE   You're not above the law, Mr. Stuart.

STUART   Please. Call me David.

ROSE   You're not above the law, David.

STUART   I'm innocent. What crime have I committed?

ROSE   You stole something.

STUART   I never stole anything in my life.

ROSE   Look, I was born with a gift, okay? I have a voice. I can use my music to touch people, and I've spent my life learning how to do that. When I stand in front of a crowd, or one of my songs or videos gets played, well I hope I help everybody share feelings... sometimes feelings about love. That's what a performer does. When you snatch that feeling out of the air and say, "This belongs to me"— you're stealing something from everybody I'm trying to share those feelings with. You're a thief.

STUART   No, Rose, our love is more pure and meaningful than anything all those anonymous people will ever know. It exists on a higher plane. Maybe... maybe the system will drag us down but I know our love—

ROSE   Stop it, Mr. Stuart. Just stop it. *(pause)* You are in love with a person that doesn't exist.

   STUART shakes his head.

STUART   Rose, you exist.

ROSE   I'm a married woman. I have two children and I'm very happy.

STUART   Come on, Rose, you know those children don't exist.

ROSE   What?

STUART   They're symbolic.

ROSE   My children are not symbols! They are flesh and blood. I love them more than this world and I am terrified when I hear you talk about them like that!

STUART   Why are you pretending to be afraid of me?

ROSE   I *am* afraid of you! You make me afraid to walk down the street! You make me afraid to meet my fans after a show! *(pause)* You make me afraid to sing.

STUART   Rose, you're not being fair.

ROSE   Fair? You come in here and talk about me and my family as if we're all some kind of… of… projection. We aren't. We are real. We have feelings!

STUART   I HAVE FEELINGS TOO! *(pause)* I… I'm sorry. I didn't mean to… I love you, Rose.

ROSE   Look, David… if you really love me then you've got to believe me when I tell you the truth.

STUART   I will.

ROSE   Okay. *(beat)* The truth is: I do not love you. I'm sorry you got hurt.

There is a pause. Lights dim on ROSE as she exits.

SCENE THIRTY-FIVE: NEVER DOUBT I LOVE

Underscoring begins for the intro to "Never Doubt I Love."

STUART   My heart can't be broken anymore. It really is over. The thing is, she's just not the same girl I fell in love with. And that's the saddest truth of the whole affair. *(beat)* Of course she's not to blame. We're all buffeted in the gale, and as hard as we try, nothing stays the same. But for one brief moment we were together—in the eye of the storm—the whole chaotic world whirling around us and… and then she was gone. Her heart was swept away. *(beat)* When I was eighteen I got a place on a gypsum boat sailing for Brazil. A great adventure. But more than all the ports of the southern seas, the nights wandering the streets of Rio de Janeiro, what I remember most was standing on the aft deck that first day out. I'd spent my whole young life puttering around the stretch of shore where I grew up but that was the first time I ever saw "her sea-bound coast" slip beneath the horizon. The saddest sight in the world. The soft grey fog wrapped around us and… my home was gone. It's hard to keep your perspective out there. Everything sounds different, the shoosh of the water on your bows, an invisible seabird crying somewhere high above… standing watch one night, hundreds of miles out, I thought I heard the bump and pull of oars, I strained into the fog and

I saw... a lone dory man paying out a long line from a boat he'd built with his own hands, a vision from a hundred years ago that was there... and then was gone. *(beat)* The mind tries to hold what it needs and that can be a miracle. But when everything is drowned in time and distance, a little thing like love... it can disappear.

> Slowly, STUART packs up his briefcase as ROSE sings *"Never Doubt I Love."*

ROSE

In an age of troubles
In an age of uncertainty
In an age of dwindling hope
You still have me

No matter where you are
No matter how far from home
No matter if you're lost
You still have me

Doubt that the stars are fire
Doubt that the earth doth move
Doubt truth to be a liar
But never doubt I love
Never doubt I love

You may lose things dear to you
You may feel naked and alone
You may think you're losing your faith
But you still have me

Remember when you're tired
Remember when you're defeated
They can take all your dreams
But you still have me...

Doubt that the stars are fire
Doubt that the earth doth move
Doubt truth to be a liar
But never doubt I love
Never doubt I love

> *Instrumental solo.*

> STUART *begins to exit then stops, looking back at* ROSE.
> *It's as if the song was written just for him.*

Doubt that the stars are fire
Doubt that the earth doth move
Doubt truth to be a liar
But never doubt I love
Never doubt I love
Never doubt I love

I know your pain I won't pretend
Serve God, love me, and mend

> ROSE *finishes the song. Lights fade to black.* "Ding."

> The End.

SONG CREDITS

"Wilma or a Betty Man" by Melanie Doane and Rick Neigher, Prairie Ocean South and Sylvan St. Songs

"She's Like A Swallow" – traditional

"The Mermaid of Port Mouton" by Paul Ledoux

"Saltwater" by Melanie Doane, M. Doane Music, Sony / ATV Music Publishing Canada

"Goliath" by Melanie Doane and Rick Neigher, Sony / ATV Music Publishing Canada, Sylvan St. Songs

"Adam's Rib" by Melanie Doane and Rick Neigher, Sony / ATV Music Publishing Canada, Sylvan St. Songs

"Waiting For The Tide To Turn" by Melanie Doane and Rick Neigher, Sony / ATV Music Publishing Canada, Sylvan St. Songs

"Farewell To Nova Scotia" – traditional

"Still Desire You" by Melanie Doane and Rick Neigher, Prairie Ocean South and Sylvan St. Songs

"I Can't Take My Eyes Off You" by Melanie Doane and Kevin Fox, Sony / ATV Music Publishing Canada, Kevin Fox

"Happy Homemaker" by Melanie Doane and Rick Neigher, Sony / ATV Music Publishing Canada and Sylvan St. Songs

"Bionic" by Melanie Doane and Rick Neigher, Prairie Ocean South, Sylvan St. Songs

"Never Doubt I Love" by Ted Dykstra, Prairie Ocean South

All songs used by permission.

FIRE

Fire premiered in April 1985 at Magnus Theatre, Thunder Bay, Ontario, with the following company:

CALE BLACKWELL	Peter Willson
HERCHEL BLACKWELL	Jerry Franken
MOLLY KING	Janet Land
TRUMAN KING	John Dolan
J.D. BLACKWELL, SHELLY GRANT, JAMES, DAVE	Michael Fawkes

Director: Brian Richmond
Musical Director: David Smyth
Set and Costume Design: John Dinning
Lighting Design: Peter Smith

CHARACTERS

Ages are listed for the time the play begins.

CALE BLACKWELL: seventeen, good looking, an excellent piano player

HERCHEL BLACKWELL: eighteen, handsome, serious

J.D. BLACKWELL: forty-five, a widower, an old-time country preacher

MOLLY KING: fourteen, blooming, innocent and curious

TRUMAN KING: thirty, desperate, broke, insecure and entirely wired to the American dream

SHELLY GRANT: middle-aged borscht-belt TV comic

JAMES: forty-ish, gay, "born again" makeup man

SAM: late thirties, hotshot Northern media coach

JACKSON: forty-ish Texan convict, country music fan

SET NOTES

There are twenty-three scenes in *Fire*, set in almost as many locations. To accommodate the rapid changes in location it is imperative that the set be simple and that shifts between scenes be both fast and fluid. The script is designed to facilitate rapid set changes and the action should be nearly continuous.

In the original production a unit set based on the interior of an old country church was used as a connective image for the play. Minimal set elements were added to suggest specific locations. The overall look was not unlike a classic Shakespearean stage: the majority of the action took place in the central playing area, which featured a modest thrust into the audience. The bridge scene and some of the secondary action took place on an elevated platform and the band was placed upstage behind a sliding scrim.

ACT ONE

SCENE ONE

Sunday, August 25, 1957. The Assembly of God Church,
Razor Back, Arkansas.

J.D. BLACKWELL, the preacher, leads the singing of "Bright
Morning Stars." His son HERCHEL stands in one pew.
HERCHEL's younger brother CALE plays the piano.
TRUMAN KING stands in another pew, beaming at his
daughter MOLLY, who stands close to BLACKWELL.

CAST *Bright morning stars are rising*
Bright morning stars are rising
Bright morning stars are rising
Bright morning stars are rising
Day is a-breaking in my soul

Oh where are our dear brothers?
Oh where are our dear brothers?
They are gone to heaven, the sheltered
Day is a-breaking in my soul

Bright morning stars are rising
Bright morning stars are rising
Bright morning stars are rising
Bright morning stars are rising
Day is a-breaking in my soul

The song ends. MOLLY steps forward, opens her Bible
and reads.

MOLLY Hebrews, Chapter 12:29 to 13:2: "Our God is a consuming fire. Let brotherly love continue. Be not forgetful to entertain strangers: for thereby some have entertained angels unawares."

BLACKWELL Thank you, Molly. Very nice. You know, brothers and sisters, when I look in the papers I marvel at how fast this old world is changing. Seems like a truck, brakes gone, careening down Jacob's mountain. The speed that this world is travelling has got people worked up. Folks are coming to me and saying: "J.D. we're afraid. The coloureds are taking over our schools and we're afraid."

"The communists are getting stronger all the time, and we are afraid." "There's a radioactive cloud up in the sky, J.D., from the A-bomb tests out there in Nevada. Poison is raining down all over Arkansas and we are afraid."

MOLLY   Sometimes... when I get to thinking about you, Jesus, it's as if you take me by the hand and lead me to a private place where just the two of us can be alone together.

You see, my daddy gave me this illustrated Bible and I've been looking at the pictures in it by the hour. I swear you are as handsome as Gary Cooper, who is my most favourite movie star.

> As BLACKWELL preaches, the congregation, especially TRUMAN KING, add "Amen," "Praise the Lord," etc.

BLACKWELL   You don't need to be afraid of the Negroes. You don't need to be afraid of the communists. You don't need to be afraid of the radioactive cloud. Brothers and sisters, all you need to be afraid of is the righteous anger of God! "For our God is a consuming fire!"

MOLLY   It's your eyes more than anything else. They are so calm and... and so powerful. I can tell from them that you are not at all stuck-up about how special you are.

BLACKWELL   Satan wants you afraid of these worldly trials. He wants you to forget brotherly love, but God says, "Let brotherly love continue!"

MOLLY   It's like you was the smartest, most handsome man in the entire world and all you wanted to do was stand by the roadside and fix flat tires for total strangers.

BLACKWELL   Satan, he doesn't see it that way. He wants you so full of fear about the troubles of this world that you can't see the other kingdom.

MOLLY   The menfolk who run our Assembly of God Church here in Razor Back... all they ever talk about is being afraid. You aren't afraid of anything, are you, Jesus?

BLACKWELL   Because when you forget the other kingdom, brothers and sisters, you are on the highway to hell!

MOLLY   My daddy, Truman King, is real afraid. He's been out of work since Momma died, and he says if we don't get a miracle soon we'll just have to walk away and let the bank take over our mobile home. When he talks like that I get scared too.

BLACKWELL   I tell you folks, I look around this town, many of you aren't entertaining the angels.

MOLLY   See, Jesus, the thing is… the thing is… I'm a woman now. When it happened I got so scared, and Haddy McPhee, she said it was the curse put on Eve by the Lord God Jehovah!

BLACKWELL   I know Satan is in some of your houses. I can see his tail sticking out of the chimney.

MOLLY   But sometimes I get these… feelings. I mean, I look at the kids I was out playing with just last week and they seem like babies to me.

BLACKWELL   You know what Satan's tail looks like? It looks like a TV antenna.

MOLLY   When I get scared I try and imagine what it would be like if *you* showed up in our town. Mostly you walk around like Gary Cooper, but other times you're just like a normal person.

BLACKWELL   You're sitting there proud of that TV you can finally afford—proud of that new car in the driveway. Proud of yourselves, ain't ya?

MOLLY   Like Reverend Blackwell's boys. Herchel, he's as quiet and deep as an underground river and Cale, he's like a fountain splashing up to the sun. They're like different melodies sung at the same time. You know how good that can feel. Truth is, I don't know which of them I think is the cutest. They are both special. Brave, like you.

BLACKWELL   You're forgetting Jesus! He is the way. He is the truth. He is your salvation, and without his grace you will burn eternally in hellfire! And the only thing that is gonna save you from that blistering inferno of everlasting boiling flesh is the sacred fire of the Holy Ghost himself. Now, you think on that while Truman King, my boy Herchel and the ladies of the auxiliary take up the collection.

>*MOLLY and HERCHEL get the collection plates off the top of the piano. CALE overhears the dialogue below.*

HERCHEL (*whisper*) Hi Molly.

MOLLY (*whisper*) Hi Herchel. (*sniffs*) Mmmm, what have you got in your hair?

HERCHEL Ah, I don't know... soap.

MOLLY Smells real nice.

BLACKWELL And while they are passing the plate, my son Cale will play a sacred song he's been practising up for you. Now remember, it doesn't matter what you give, just so long as it comes from the heart. It's all the same in the eyes of the Lord.

>*CALE begins to play "Swing Down Chariot." Collection is taken in the audience. At first the song is straight gospel, with the congregation joining in. But as he plays, CALE can't help but notice MOLLY and HERCHEL having a lot of fun singing together. So he starts to rock the beat, trying to get MOLLY's attention. Following CALE's lead, MOLLY changes how she's singing—it starts to sound a little bit like rock and roll. MOLLY leads all the younger folks in a doo-wop part, leaving the older members singing the straighter parts. TRUMAN KING is particularly impressed by what he hears, even dancing a little step with his hand over his head in testimony. Everybody enjoys his music—except BLACKWELL.*

CALE & CONGREGATION Why don't you swing down chariot
Stop and let me ride
Swing down chariot, stop and let me ride
Rock me low, and rock me low
And rock me easy
I got a home on the other side

MOLLY & HERCHEL *Swing, swing, swing (continues under)*

CALE   *Ezekiel went down to the middle of a field*
Saw two angels working on a chariot wheel
He wasn't too particular 'bout working on the wheel
Just wanted to see how the chariot would feel

ALL   *Why don't you swing down chariot*
Stop and let me ride
Swing down chariot, stop and let me ride
Rock me low, and rock me low
And rock me easy
I got a home on the other side.

CALE   *Well, well, well, I got a father in the promised land*

MOLLY & HERCHEL   *(under) Do ah, bop bop bop, do ah, bop bop bop*

CALE   *And I ain't gonna be happy till I shake his hand.*

MOLLY & HERCHEL   *(under) Do ah, bop bop bop, do ah, bop bop bop*

CALE   *Rock me low, and rock me low, and rock me easy*
Well I got a home on the other side

CALE & CONGREGATION   *Why don't you swing down chariot,*
Stop and let me ride
Swing down chariot, stop and let me ride
Rock me low, and rock me low
And rock me easy
I got a home on the other side.

> CALE *is really rocking by the last line. He finishes strong, with hoots from the crowd.* KING *gathers up the collection plates, impressed by the take, but* BLACKWELL *scowls.*

BLACKWELL   *(whispers)* Boy, have you lost your ever lovin' mind? *(to congregation)* Pray for my son, and I'll see you next Sunday.

> *As the congregation leaves,* KING *brings the collection plates to* BLACKWELL.

KING   Now that is what I call an offering. That brother of yours has real talent, Herchel.

HERCHEL Yes sir, and I must tell you I admired the way your daughter read the scripture today.

MOLLY *(excited)* Did you really?

HERCHEL I sure did, especially that part about "entertaining angels unawares."

CALE Molly *is* an angel unaware.

> *CALE noodles on the piano. MOLLY moves to stand beside him.*

KING So... Herchel, tell me, you joining the Brotherhood of the South this year?

HERCHEL I don't think my daddy much likes the idea, sir.

KING Why not, Reverend?

BLACKWELL Because it is nothing more than a Sunday drinking club playing at politics.

KING Reverend, that organization stands for all that is decent and gallant in white Southern manhood and everybody knows it. And they sure as heck support this church. Look at this. Right off the bus. *(takes a small box out of his pocket and opens it)*

> *KING takes a transistor radio out of the box. He hands the radio to BLACKWELL.*

I have been able to purchase a sizable consignment of these little gems all the way from New York City.

BLACKWELL Zeco "Satellite Radios"?

KING Transistor radios are all the rage up north. And the Brothers have agreed to sell 'em door to door—all proceeds to go to this church. With any luck, every kid in Arkansas will want one of these units.

BLACKWELL And what are they going to listen to?

KING Why, music. You know... popular music.

BLACKWELL I swear, Truman, it's like you didn't hear a word of my sermon.

> *BLACKWELL hands the radio back to KING and walks off with the collection funds. KING hands the radio to HERCHEL.*

KING   There's religious shows on the radio, too.

HERCHEL   Yes sir, I heard 'em.

MOLLY   You know any Elvis songs?

CALE   *(dismissive)* Elvis. I write my own stuff.

KING   You'll talk to him, won't you? Don't want to get stuck with these things, and hell, with a little enterprise we could get this church out of debt.

HERCHEL   Yes sir.

MOLLY   Rock and roll? I don't believe you for a minute.

CALE   Oh, yeah, well just you listen.

HERCHEL   Earphones in the box?

KING   Earphones? *(looks in the box)*

HERCHEL   Can't hear anything without 'em.

KING   Them Yankee bastards.

> *CALE has the tune. He sings "Devil In Her Eyes."
> MOLLY, delighted, starts dancing. KING likes what he hears.*

CALE   *Good golly gosh gee*
Won't you listen to me
I want to bop, bop bop bop bop
And I hope you'll agree

HERCHEL   Cale, Daddy's gonna be back in a second.

CALE   *Oh Lord I'm gonna pray*
Some day I'm gonna have my way
My baby's an angel
And she's gonna marry me

My baby's an angel
And she's so fine
Here's why I love her and I won't lie

> *My baby's an angel*
> *Got the devil in her eyes*

BLACKWELL   (*enters*) Boy!

> *CALE stops.*

Cale, how many times I got to tell you, that kind of music has no place in the house of God.

CALE   It's only a song, Daddy, besides, ain't nobody here but us.

BLACKWELL   God is here. That music is of the flesh, not the spirit. It is not Christian.

CALE   Damn it, Daddy, I am as Christian-minded as you, and you know it.

KING   Well, Reverend, we best be going. Come on, Molly.

> *MOLLY and KING start to exit. HERCHEL tries to follow.*

HERCHEL   Mr. King, you forgot your radio.

BLACKWELL   Herchel! Pray with your brother.

> *HERCHEL catches MOLLY's eye, then, embarrassed, looks away.*

Cale, you kneel down and you pray to the Lord Jesus Christ to take that pride out of your soul.

> *CALE kneels. HERCHEL kneels. MOLLY and KING exit. BLACKWELL opens his Bible.*

Chapter 8, First Corinthians. "Knowledge puffeth up, but love edifieth." Herchel, verse 2.

HERCHEL   "And if any man think that he knoweth any thing, he knoweth nothing yet as he ought to know."

BLACKWELL   Cale. Luke 18, verse 14.

CALE   "Suffer the little children to come unto me"?

BLACKWELL   That's 16. Herchel.

HERCHEL   "For every one that exalteth himself shall be abased; and he that humbleth himself shall be exalted."

BLACKWELL   Cale, if you spent less time at that piano and more time with your Bible, maybe you'd keep in mind the Lord's plan for—

CALE   I know where my talent comes from, Daddy, and I don't need reminding about the Lord's plan!!

BLACKWELL   I do! *(beat)* Look, son, I know what you got inside of you. It's in me, too.

CALE   You don't know nothing about me, that's plain.

BLACKWELL   When I was your age, I went rampaging down to New Orleans. Spent six months getting low as a snake. It did me no good and it broke my mother's heart.

CALE   I'm a full-grown man. I got to wrassle my own demons.

BLACKWELL   Not if it means dragging them into my church.

HERCHEL   Daddy, the only other place in town with a piano is Pinetop's.

BLACKWELL   No son of mine plays in a whorehouse!

CALE   Damn it, Daddy, I can't play in *your* church—I can't play at Pinetop's. Where the hell can I play?

BLACKWELL   If you think—

CALE   I do, Daddy. I do think! It scares you when I do my own thinking, don't it? You afraid I'm gonna find out about something you want to pretend don't even exist.

BLACKWELL   I swear, sometimes I look at you and I don't see my son.

CALE   What do you see?

BLACKWELL   A sheep-killin' dog.

CALE starts to leave.

You are going to Bible college, boy, and they will beat that pride out of you. Hear me?

CALE   Yeah, I hear you.

CALE exits. BLACKWELL looks at HERCHEL.

BLACKWELL   You go talk to him, Herchel…

HERCHEL   What do I say? You made him look a fool in front of Molly and Mr. King, and you did the same to me.

BLACKWELL   Now don't you start, boy.

HERCHEL   No sir. I got nothing to say in this matter.

> *HERCHEL exits.*

BLACKWELL   What are you doing, Lord? What are you doing?

> *BLACKWELL pounds the piano top and exits.*

SCENE TWO

> *Sunday night, August 25, 1957. Outside Pinetop's, a black bar near a railway trestle, Razor Back, Arkansas.*
>
> *Dirty blues music underscores: CALE and HERCHEL run on, both dishevelled and laughing. HERCHEL has a bottle of booze. He takes a drink.*

HERCHEL   I swear, Jimmy Jones don't get a better lock on his back door, I'm gonna turn into a souse.

CALE   Daddy gonna catch you and whip your ass first.

HERCHEL   You keep on playing that boogie-woogie in church, he'll die of a heart attack long before he gets my britches down.

CALE   It'll take a lot more than Daddy to cut my water off, Herchel.

HERCHEL   I truly don't understand why you torment him so.

CALE   I torment him? He's been tormenting me since the day I was born.

HERCHEL   Bullshit. He always treated both of us decent and you know it.

CALE   That's okay for you to say. You got the room with the window.

> *HERCHEL laughs. He hands CALE the bottle.*

Growing up in a closet make anybody want to bust out—

BOTH   —and boogie!

> *They laugh again. CALE drinks and hands HERCHEL the bottle.*

HERCHEL   You know what? You sounded great this morning.

CALE   I was great! Did you see the look on Daddy's face? Think he dropped a load in his drawers.

HERCHEL   Now, Cale, you can't be talking about him like that. He's a religious man. Besides, if he's right, Jesus doesn't much like your taste in music.

CALE   Herchel, I learned to play piano in two weeks. It is a God-given gift.

HERCHEL   Well, I sure as hell don't know about that.

CALE   Well, I sure as hell do. Come on.

> *CALE heads towards the front door of Pinetop's.*

HERCHEL   Where do you think you're going?

CALE   I am gonna slide on into Pinetop's and sit in with that band.

HERCHEL   *(laughs)* You can't play in a whorehouse.

> *CALE gives HERCHEL a "you want to bet" look.*

Well, if you're going in there, I'm going with you.

CALE   You confuse me, big brother! One minute you all hot on the salvation of my soul, the next you jumping up and down to go into a whorehouse in darkie town. *(laughs)* You hot, boy. You want it.

HERCHEL   Which "it" you mean?

CALE   Herchel, you're dying for a little taste of what a woman's got to give.

HERCHEL   You're no different.

CALE   Oh yeah, well all you're doing is lookin' and thinkin'— I already done the deed.

HERCHEL   Bullshit. Who?

CALE   You got saliva in the corner of your mouth, Herchel, you droolin'.

HERCHEL   Come on, Cale. What're you talking about?

CALE   Blond gal heard the killer playing off the back of a pickup over at the fairgrounds. Next thing I knew it's dark, I'm on top of her and she is writhing around like a shot snake.

HERCHEL   Where?

CALE   Wet grass out behind Bailey's Mill. Didn't even take my shoes off.

HERCHEL   I don't believe you for a second.

CALE   Where you think I got these grass stains then? *(points to his knees)* These pants ain't never goin' near a wash. They're holy relics now.

HERCHEL   You're lyin'.

CALE   Yeah, I'm lyin'.

> They look at each other for a moment.

HERCHEL   So, what was it like?

CALE   Like pounding a piano harder than it can be done. You never heard such grunting and groaning in your life. Know what else she done?

HERCHEL   What?

CALE   She sucked my ear.

HERCHEL   Sucked your ear.

CALE   Tongue hanging out to here… panting like an animal.

HERCHEL   Holy shit, aren't you scared of what's gonna happen?

CALE   God'll probably make my dick fall off, is all. *(pause)* What are you looking at me like that for? Man, you are serious as cancer.

HERCHEL You are supposed to be coming with me to Beaumont Bible College next week, and there you stand bragging on your lustful sins.

CALE And there you stand drinking sour mash you stole out of the back of Jimmy Jones's store.

HERCHEL There is a hell of a lot of difference between stealing a bottle of whiskey and swimming in slime.

CALE Jesus, sometimes you sound so much like Daddy I could puke.

HERCHEL You gonna stick with Jesus?

CALE Yeah, I'm gonna stick with Jesus. He's my Saviour and my Lord just like he's always been, just like he's always gonna be.

HERCHEL I want you to make a pact that you won't let Jesus down.

CALE I'll make any kind of pact you want and double it.

> *HERCHEL hauls out a knife.*

What in hell is that for?

HERCHEL If we do it, we do it for real.

CALE Any way you want.

> *HERCHEL pricks CALE's thumb, then cuts his own.*

HERCHEL Now you taste mine and I taste yours.

CALE Why, Herchel, I swear, this *is* ungodly.

HERCHEL Not if it gets you on that bus to Beaumont.

> *HERCHEL tastes CALE's blood, CALE tastes his.*

CALE Aunt Haddy told me that when you do this with somebody you are responsible for each other's soul forever and any time you get asked your most awful secret by the one who shares the blood, you got to tell 'em or you both go straight to hell.

HERCHEL Okay, that's the way you want it, let's mix it up.

> *HERCHEL and CALE put their thumbs together.*

Now say after me: I promise...

CALE   I promise...

HERCHEL To be with Jesus in the hereafter.

CALE   To be with Jesus in the hereafter—and with my brother in the here and now.

HERCHEL And with my brother in the here and now.

CALE   And remember this night for as long as I live.

HERCHEL And remember this night for as long as I live—so help me God.

CALE   So help me God.

> *Pause. Music begins to build in Pinetop's.*

So? You want to know what my most awful secret is?

HERCHEL I already know.

CALE   These grass stains are nothing, Truman King gave me this, this afternoon. Latest issue of *Country Round-up Magazine*. Page twenty-seven.

> *CALE hands HERCHEL a rolled up magazine he's had tucked up under his belt.*

See, I'm not going to Beaumont. I'm going to Memphis.

HERCHEL Memphis? What the—

CALE   Mr. King got a second cousin working for Sun Records. He believes he can get that boy to give the meat man a listen.

HERCHEL Oh, I see. Truman King is now managing careers in the music business.

CALE   He knows enough to believe his ears. *(points at a picture of Elvis in the magazine)* Elvis's first record went to number one. See that pink Caddy? He *owns* that.

> *HERCHEL tosses the magazine back at CALE.*

HERCHEL Maybe he owns that Cadillac, but who owns his soul?

CALE   Don't preach at me, Herchel.

HERCHEL   Think practical, boy. Where you gonna get the money to go to Memphis?

CALE   Truman is selling off his mobile home. He's bankrolling me and he's gonna manage my career.

HERCHEL   Bankroll you? Manage you? Cale, that man has been living on a wing and a prayer for nearly two years.

CALE   Truman King could smell a dollar bill under a truckload of pig shit, and come tomorrow, Truman and me will be on the Memphis Flyer, rolling over this here bridge and on into glory.

HERCHEL   You're not going to Memphis, you're going to hell.

CALE   You're whistling out your ass, Herchel.

> *CALE boosts himself up on the girders and starts to climb to the top of the trestle.*

HERCHEL   What you think you're doin'?

CALE   Goin' to the top, brother. That's what life is all about.

HERCHEL   This life is just a way station.

CALE   Face it, Herchel, Memphis beats the dirt out of Daddy's little toll booth on the road to heaven.

HERCHEL   Cale Blackwell, you've been breaking our daddy's heart ever since the day Mama died. You keep this up and you will burn for eternity.

CALE   Eternity! Man, you don't even know what that word means!

HERCHEL   I'm leaving for Beaumont and I expect you on that bus beside me.

> *HERCHEL makes as if to leave.*

CALE   Herchel! I'm calling in our blood oath, right now. Get on up here.

HERCHEL   Up there? You're nuts.

CALE   "With my brother in the here and now." That was your oath, Herchel. That was your sacred oath.

HERCHEL I'll see your blood oath and raise you two.

> *HERCHEL climbs the trestle. He's nervous.*

CALE There's something we got to do, Herchel. You stick with me and I'm on that bus with you. You can't cut it and I'm Memphis bound. That sound fair?

HERCHEL Fair enough. What if another train comes by?

> *CALE offers him his hand. HERCHEL takes it and CALE pulls him up on to the trestle.*

CALE We sprout wings and fly, brother. Come on, I want to show you something. Look down, Herchel. Ain't but a hundred feet. See, the difference between you and me is that you got this idea eternity is somewhere over in the next county.

HERCHEL It's not in this world, Cale.

CALE Where is it then? Twenty-five years down the road when you fall outta your rocking chair? It's right here. Right now.

> *CALE forces HERCHEL to look straight down.*

Look it in the eye, brother.

> *HERCHEL is transfixed.*

HERCHEL It makes me too dizzy! I can't look.

CALE *(laughing)* And I can't look away.

> *CALE spreads his arms as if getting ready to swan dive.*

I'm gonna hit the surface of eternity so clean there won't be a ripple.

HERCHEL Don't, Cale. You're drunk.

CALE Whoaaa—

> *CALE pretends to fall but lands comfortably on the lip of the bridge. He takes a long drink and points down.*

That's the drop. That's the black nothin'. Maybe that's all we were born to. You ever think about that, Herchel?

HERCHEL Yeah, Cale, I do.

CALE Scares the hell out of me.

HERCHEL Me too.

CALE Scares Daddy half to death if you ask me, but all he wants us to do is look away and pretend it isn't there.

HERCHEL It's just another temptation to despair. Best thing you can do is look away.

CALE The hell it is. Come on, we gonna walk rail right over into Tennessee.

> *CALE gets up and balances himself on the rail.*
> *HERCHEL backs away.*

Hey, where you goin'?

HERCHEL I'll let you play this game by yourself. I think that's the way you like it best.

> *CALE jumps to his feet.*

CALE We got an oath, you son of a bitch! You gotta stand by me!

HERCHEL Stay away from me, Cale!

CALE You got to face it, Herchel. Face the black nothing. You can't do that, no God will think you're worth savin'. You got to crawl on your belly into that stinking pit and spit in Satan's face.

> *HERCHEL backs away too quickly and loses his balance.*
> *He starts to fall, CALE grabs him by the wrist.*
> *HERCHEL is hanging over the edge.*

HERCHEL I'm gonna fall! I'm—Lord Jesus! I can't hold on! I'm gonna fall!

CALE Shut up, you son of a bitch! I got you!

> *CALE strengthens his grip. He's sure HERCHEL will not fall. HERCHEL is still in terror.*

Hey, now's the time I got to know.

HERCHEL Know what?

CALE   Your most awful secret. Tell me—if you don't tell me, maybe I'm gonna let go... maybe you'll die, right now, in sin!

HERCHEL My most awful secret is...

CALE   What?

HERCHEL I lust after...

CALE   Tell it, brother.

HERCHEL I lust after Molly King!

> *CALE laughs and hauls HERCHEL up.*

CALE   Molly King! Why you dirty old man. Swing your leg over here, you Molly-loving fool. That's right. Molly. Golly. Shucks! Mmmmm yeah, wouldn't half mind a taste of that myself.

> *CALE dances down the trestle, laughing. HERCHEL stares at him, angry but still in shock.*

What are you looking at me like that for, man? I saved you, didn't I? Your ass was hung right out over eternity and I saved it!

> *CALE starts laughing again.*

HERCHEL Your soul is in trouble, Cale Blackwell. I'm going to pray for it.

CALE   You'd better pray for yourself, brother. Lustin' after that little girl.

> *CALE runs off down the trestle, howling like a train.*

HERCHEL Don't you worry, boy. I won't stumble, I won't stray from the path! Jesus keeps me from temptation. He holds me up! I don't have Satan in my soul. I'm not like you! Not like you!

SCENE THREE

Saturday night, February 15, 1958. The Dew Drop Inn, Lubbock, Texas.

> *CALE is playing "The Joint Is Really Rockin'" with*
> *a small band.*

CALE   *The joint is really rockin'*
The joint is really rockin' tonight
The joint is really burnin'
The joint is really churnin' tonight
Come on pretty baby
The joint is really rockin' tonight

The joint is really rockin'
The joint is really rockin' tonight
The joint is catchin' fire
The joint is really rockin' tonight
Come on pretty baby
The joint is really boppin' tonight

We gonna get real gone
Gonna have a ball
Gonna tear the roof
Off this union hall
Dance all night
Stomp and shout
Gonna show 'em all
What it's all about

> *Break.*

> *Lights dim on CALE. Music vamps. Special on MOLLY*
> *who runs on at the trestle level.*

MOLLY   I—I—Jesus, I just... I been... I saw... well, we been out on
the road for months now and I never get to see Cale play,
so I... I... I have been in a barroom, Jesus! I snuck in
and... and you won't believe what happened. Cale's up
there on stage just going crazy and all around him there's
this big crowd of women, and I do mean women, Jesus!
Women old enough to be my mama, all hot eyes and
mussed hair, crowded up there screaming at the top of
their lungs... and then... this big blond woman, she rips
off her panties and throws them at Cale! The place went
wild. 'Fore you knew it the stage is covered in panties
and that blond woman is climbing up on the piano and—

and... she's... it was a powerful thing, and Cale was doin' it all, up there howling and beating on the piano with the heel of his boot!

> *CALE hits a high note with the heel of his boot. Music stops.*

Man, it was great!

> *MOLLY dances. Lights back up on CALE.*

CALE   *Baby come on out a-dancin'*
The joint is really rockin' tonight
I said baby come on out a-dancin'
The joint is really rockin' tonight
Come on pretty baby
The joint is really rockin' tonight

SCENE FOUR

> *Sunday morning, February 16, 1958. The studio, WWVI Radio, Beaumont, Texas.*

> *The PINE FAMILY, an old-fashioned gospel group, sings "Salvation Highway."*

THE PINES   *If you're travellin'*
On salvation highway
Put your faith in the Lord
No matter where you roam
And keep your Bible
Right there beside you
It is the road map
Gonna guide you home

> *As THE PINES play, lights shift to reveal HERCHEL pacing around the studio running over his notes. There is a comic tone to his nervousness as he begins testing the microphone.*

PINE SINGER   Thank you, we are The Pines and we will be right back with Reverend Blackwell.

PRODUCER   *(from control booth)* Okay, Reverend. We're live in sixty seconds.

HERCHEL   Testing, testing. One, two, three… one-two-three.

PRODUCER   Herchel, you're crowding the mic again.

HERCHEL   Sorry.

PRODUCER   Just try and relax and talk normal when we go on air.

HERCHEL   Yes, sir.

PRODUCER   Try it again.

> *HERCHEL grabs the mic chord by mistake and unplugs it. He shoves it back in, then drops his notes. He stoops to pick them up and bangs his head on the mic stand. He clears his throat and goes into a fast mumble.*

HERCHEL   Praise the Lord. Good evening brothers and sisters, and welcome to *The Old Time Gospel Hour.* This is the Reverend Berchel Hackwell… Herchel—

PRODUCER   You're swallowing your words.

HERCHEL   I'm sorry.

PRODUCER   They told me you were the best they had over there at the college.

HERCHEL   There is a—a heck of a lot of difference between doing this in class and going live to air.

PRODUCER   Well you know what they say, son: "Money talks and bullshit walks." Thirty seconds.

HERCHEL   Could they maybe just play an extra song instead?

PRODUCER   You gonna pay for that?

HERCHEL   I can't seem to collect my thoughts.

PRODUCER   Never mind your thoughts. People tune in for preachin'—hot preachin', so if you've got a pecker you better get it up.

HERCHEL   Look mister, I know the kind of filth you play all week long on this station. I hear it and I hate it, but this is the Sabbath, and when this show is on air this studio is a church. There are people out there in need of God's love, so you just keep your foul mouth out of the house of the Lord, you—you take your wiseassed, money-grubbing mind and you shove it down into the stinking pit of hell where it belongs! Keep it out of the house of the Lord!

PRODUCER   That's the stuff, Reverend. Give 'em hell.

HERCHEL   *(realizes he's been set up—and it worked)* Let's go.

> THE PINES *kick in—a full up-tempo bluegrass version of "Salvation Highway."*

THE PINES   *Keep travellin' on salvation's highway*
Dodge the devil's detours
And trust the Master's plan
One day you'll stand
On a mighty mountain
And down below
You'll see the promised land

SCENE FIVE

> *Sunday afternoon, May 11, 1958. An audition hall, New York, New York.*

> MOLLY *is sprawled on a bench reading an Archie comic.* TRUMAN KING *paces the room.*

CALE   What in God's name is wrong with that Sullivan jerk anyway! *(takes a drink)*

KING   Ah Sullivan, what does he know?

CALE   "Guitar acts"! Elvis could come in here right now and plug his guitar in and play till his fingers fell off. He couldn't do what I do on this piano. He couldn't do *that*. God gave it to me, nobody else.

KING   I know that, boy.

CALE   Then how come you can't get me on the TV!

KING   I will. I will get you on TV.

CALE   Those records go nowhere outside the South 'less you do.

KING This guy from "The Shelly Grant Show" is—

CALE Shelly Grant is a horse's ass.

KING He is the king of comedy, Cale. He gets behind us, we are in.

CALE This don't work, Truman, I'm goin' home.

LACKEY (off) Yes, studio six. Truman King and Cale Blackwell. Yes sir...

There is a knock on the door. KING rushes to it.

KING Watch me, boy. Molly, sit up! We got a TV guy coming in here.

CALE pulls on an oversize white dinner jacket. MOLLY sits up, pats her hair and pulls down her dress. KING opens the door. SHELLY GRANT is standing there.

Shelly Grant. I—I...

GRANT Mr. King.

KING A real honour, sir. I been watching your show for years.

MOLLY We love you down in Arkansas.

GRANT That's nice to hear.

KING I didn't—that is, we thought you'd send a producer or something.

GRANT On talent I always make the final decision.

(eyeing CALE) Is this the whole look?

KING He's quite the showman. You won't be disappointed.

GRANT I understand you don't shake.

CALE Well I...

GRANT That's correct, isn't it? He doesn't shake.

KING Hell sir, he don't need to shake. When he feels it, he just jumps up and kicks the piano stool right across the stage.

MOLLY And his legs go real stiff!

KING gives MOLLY a reproachful look.

GRANT   He kicks the stool.

CALE   Yes sir. And I've been known to dance on the keyboard, too.

GRANT   Sounds right dynamic.

KING   Look, I know you wanted a guitar act, but they're a dime a dozen these days. What we got here is something new.

GRANT   Mr. King, I can imagine what your boy delivers. The outfit, the stiff legs, the kicked stool. I'll bet he drives them wild at a catfish bake in Louisiana.

We're talking about national television.

CALE   Look man, if Elvis can do what he done on Sullivan...

GRANT   Sullivan! The man books talking mice.

CALE   Hey, I ain't no talking mouse.

KING   Cale.

CALE   The name of the game is rock and roll and it don't come from New York City.

GRANT   We've been known to develop our own talent in New York.

KING   It's going to take you five years to train some pale-blooded Yankee boy to sing like a nigger.

GRANT   We'll use Italians.

KING   Still going to take three years and by that time this whole thing will be long gone. The fact is this music comes from the South. We own it, and if we didn't, you wouldn't be here. So... do we get down to business or do I phone the Sullivan show?

> GRANT studies him. No movement. KING picks up the phone.

Yeah, I want to put through a call to CBS. Yeah, the number there is Riverside—

GRANT   I need him tonight.

> KING puts down the phone.

KING   Tonight?

GRANT   I had a last-minute cancellation.

KING   No way. This is the boy's first national appearance. What kind of promotion we gonna get together in eight hours?

GRANT   Bupkas.

KING   *(thinking on his feet)* Okay. Okay, but if he clicks I want an option on five more spots, spread over the season. You build him up, I give you an exclusive. What do you say?

> *KING offers a hand. GRANT and he shake.*

Well sir, let's go ink some contracts.

> *GRANT starts to leave. CALE stands.*

CALE   You cover the clubs.

GRANT   The clubs?

CALE   You pay for the clubs or no deal.

KING   He likes the club sandwiches from the hotel room service.

MOLLY   He had four today already.

GRANT   What the hell. I hear Sullivan pays the mouse in Gorgonzola.

> *GRANT exits, KING following.*

KING   What's that in American money?

GRANT   It's a kind of cheese.

KING   I knew that...

CALE   Whew-wee! We got that Yankee sucker by the balls.

> *MOLLY is startled.*

Pardon my French.

MOLLY   You don't have to apologize. I know what you mean.

CALE   You look at me funny sometimes. I could swear you flirtin'...

MOLLY   I could say the same thing about you.

The Canadian Stage Company and Citadel Theatre co-production of *Fire*. Photo by Cylla von Tiedemann. Ted Dykstra as Cale Blackwell and Nicole Underhay as Molly King.

> *CALE laughs and plops himself down on the couch beside MOLLY.*

CALE   Is this seat taken?

MOLLY   Not if I like the person.

CALE   How old are you again?

MOLLY   Young enough to take a chance. Old enough to know better.

CALE   You're a bewitchin' little thing, know that?

MOLLY   Maybe.

CALE   Your pappy'd love to be a fly on the wall for this.

MOLLY   I don't think so.

CALE   He'd come after me with a shotgun, wouldn't he?

MOLLY   *(laughing)* Likely as not.

CALE   I'll just tell him you made me do it.

> *MOLLY laughs and starts to tickle CALE. He tickles her back. They end up in an awkward clinch. Embarrassed, they pull apart.*

If Herchel could see this he would curl up and die.

MOLLY   What're you talking about?

CALE   'Fore we left Razor Back, Herchel told me he was sweet on you.

MOLLY   Is that so?

CALE   Herchel and me, we made a blood oath to stand by each other forever, or go straight to hell.

MOLLY   A blood oath?

CALE   See this scar? We drank each other's living blood.

MOLLY   You drank blood? They say that's how Satan seals a deal.

CALE   That's right.

MOLLY   Aren't you afraid?

CALE   I ain't scared of nothin'.

MOLLY   L-I-E—lie. You're scared every night one of them crowds goes crazy.

CALE   Oh yeah?

MOLLY   Yeah.

CALE   I like being scared.

MOLLY   Yeah, it gets you goin', don't it?

CALE   How come you know so much about it?

MOLLY   I been watchin' you since I was three. Guess I know a thing or two 'bout how you work.

CALE   Gets you going too, don't it? I see that, man, I really get goin'.

MOLLY   Tonight when you're playing I want to be right up there, on the stage.

CALE   Yeah?

MOLLY   And we'll get together after the show. Just the two of us.

CALE   What you got planned?

> *MOLLY closes her eyes for a kiss. CALE backs off.*

You better scat.

> *MOLLY is flustered.*

Nothing personal. Don't want any horses gettin' out of the barn 'fore the gig. *(with a wink)* See you when the lights go down...

> *CALE starts practising a boogie-woogie vamp. MOLLY exits.*

SCENE SIX

Sunday night, May 11, 1958. The Shelly Grant Show studio, New York, New York.

> *Lights shift. CALE is now in the TV studio playing the riff as an intro. MOLLY stands to one side watching him.*

GRANT   And now this week's pick to click. We've got a hot one for you. This time last week he was pumping piano on the back of a pickup truck in Burning Tire, Arkansas. Next week I think he'll be a star! Remember, you saw it here first! Ladies and gentlemen, that cool, crazy cat who calls himself The Killer. Mr. Cale Blackwell!

> *CALE sings "Devil In Her Eyes." MOLLY starts to dance wildly, and girls in the audience start to scream, rushing the stage and jiving in the aisles.*

CALE   *Good golly gosh gee*
Won't you listen to me
I want to bop-bop-bop-bop-bop
And I hope you'll agree
Oh Lord I'm gonna pray
Some day I'm gonna have my way
My baby's an angel
And she's gonna marry me

My baby's an angel
Oh my baby's an angel
Oh my baby's an angel
But brother let me set you wise
My baby's an angel
And she's so fine
I'll tell why I love her and I ain't lyin'
My baby's an angel
Got the devil in her eyes

(softer) I don't care what I have to do
I'd do anything to get close to you
You got everything that a good man could desire
You stole my heart
And that ain't right
Now I can't wait
Until my wedding night
Baby you're an angel
And you're gonna marry me

Let's go!

> *Piano break. CALE goes to town on the piano. MOLLY*
> *screams. The crowd goes wild.*

My baby's an angel
Oh my baby's an angel
Oh my baby's an angel
But brother let me set you wise
My baby's an angel
And she's so fine
I'll tell why I love her and I ain't lyin'
My baby's an angel
Got the devil in her eyes

My baby's an angel
Got the devil in her eyes

> *The song ends. Thunderous applause. CALE stands and*
> *bows, then staggers off.*

SCENE SEVEN

4:00 a.m., Monday, May 12, 1958. The Hotel Dixie,
New York, New York.

CALE is passed out on the bed, fully dressed. MOLLY
enters. She sits on the edge of the bed, watching CALE
intently. MOLLY gives him a tentative touch. CALE sits
bolt upright.

CALE   Wha-what?

MOLLY   *(petulant)* You said you was gonna come and see me after
the show. I waited.

CALE   Went to a party with the stagehands... Jesus, what time is
it?

MOLLY   Four in the morning. You were neat tonight. The way
your hair hung down over your face and you flipped it
back with your hand. I think I screamed.

CALE   *(laughs)* Made you feel that good, did it?

MOLLY *(flirting)* Never felt so good before.

CALE You wouldn't be thinking of takin' advantage of me now, would you little girl?

MOLLY I'm not a little girl.

> *CALE glances nervously towards KING's room.*

CALE You are my manager's shinin' pride.

> *MOLLY gives CALE an innocent peck on the cheek.*

What do you call that?

MOLLY Neckin'. *(He laughs.)* Shut up. I know as much about it as you.

CALE That so?

> *CALE grabs her by the wrist, pulls her to him and gives her a hot kiss. MOLLY pulls away.*

MOLLY You gotta do something for me 'fore I'll go any further.

CALE You name it.

> *MOLLY produces a straight razor and hands it to CALE. This takes him by surprise.*

MOLLY This is my daddy's razor. I want you to make me a blood oath, like you did with Herchel.

> *MOLLY holds out her thumb. CALE hesitates.*

CALE This here is serious stuff, Molly King. You do this and you've got to tell me your most awful secret any time I ask or go straight to hell.

MOLLY I'm ready.

CALE Tell me first.

MOLLY I want... I want to pet with you.

CALE That's a pretty awful secret, 'specially for a gal got her first pair of high heels yesterday.

MOLLY My own mama was only a year older than me when she got married, and I want to do what I want to do.

She holds out her finger. CALE cuts her gently, then casually nicks himself.

CALE Okay. Now, put 'em together and repeat after me. I promise...

MOLLY I promise...

CALE To give my soul to Cale Blackwell...

MOLLY To give my soul to Cale Blackwell...

CALE When I... when I...

MOLLY When I give him my body.

CALE whistles silently.

CALE Okay. Now we taste each other's blood.

MOLLY This is neat! *(She sucks blood from his finger.)* Mmmm. Not bad.

CALE Way I been drinkin' it should taste like wine.

CALE kisses MOLLY.

MOLLY Is this the part where you take my soul?

CALE kisses her. MOLLY slowly takes the initiative away from him. She crawls on top and starts to grind.

CALE Good golly Miss Molly!

SCENE EIGHT

Wednesday, May 27, 1959. The Assembly of God Church, Razor Back, Arkansas.

BLACKWELL goes over "Old Time Religion" with HERCHEL.

HERCHEL & BLACKWELL   *It was good for Paul and Silas*
It was good for Paul and Silas
It was good for Paul and Silas
It's good enough for me

Give me that old time religion
Give me that old time religion

Give me that old time religion
It's good enough for me

> HERCHEL *stumbles and stops.*

HERCHEL   I'm sorry, Daddy. I hit a bad note.

BLACKWELL   When you make a mistake just keep pushing on
through. Most people never notice unless you stop.
A preacher's got to know the trick of confidence.

HERCHEL   It's one thing to know that and another to feel it inside.

BLACKWELL   You'll find it when the time comes.

HERCHEL   It'll be a while before I can fill your shoes, Daddy. *(pause)*
Have you had a chance to think about my idea for the
radio broadcasts?

BLACKWELL   I have. To tell you the truth, son, I don't rightly know
how you can save a man's soul without seeing what's in
his eyes.

HERCHEL   Daddy, every time I'm on air I feel like I'm reaching right
into the homes of people who have no one else. People
who are alone and hurting. There's no other way the
word of Jesus will ever reach them.

> BLACKWELL *is about to rebut, but seeing the hurt in*
> *his son's eyes he restrains himself.*

BLACKWELL   Well, son, I sure won't stand in your way.

HERCHEL   Thank you, Daddy. You'll see, I'll make you proud.

BLACKWELL   You already have, boy. You already have.

> BLACKWELL *exits.* HERCHEL *plays "Angel Band"*
> *slowly, struggling with it.*

HERCHEL   *Oh give my longing heart to him*
Who lived and died for me
Whose blood now cleanses all from sin
And leads to victory

> *After a moment* MOLLY *enters in a garish, over-the-top*
> *outfit. A little girl playing an expensive game of dress-*
> *up. She joins in. The quality of the music becomes soulful.*

HERCHEL & MOLLY   *Oh come angel band*
Come and around me stand
Bear me away on your snow white wings
To my immortal home

> *HERCHEL stops playing, turns. For a moment he's silent, brought up short by MOLLY's outfit.*

HERCHEL   Well, look at you.

MOLLY   Sophisticated, ain't I? Hard to believe I'm just barely sixteen.

HERCHEL   My, travelling does age a person fast. Just last year you were thirteen and a half.

MOLLY   Well, I'll soon be fifteen and that's about as old as a woman needs to be. *(pause)* Feels kind of strange standing in here done up like this.

HERCHEL   It shouldn't. It should feel like home.

MOLLY   Everything's moving so fast. I'm starting to feel like my only home's in the back seat of a Cadillac car. I guess that's why it felt so good just standing here singing.

HERCHEL   I know how you feel. Down at Beaumont, I used to get so lonely. I'd lie around the dorm sick at heart, remembering the singing in this church. *(pause)* Guess maybe it was your singing I missed the most.

CALE   *(laughing)* I bet it was—you old sheep humper!

> *CALE enters dressed in an outfit even more garish than MOLLY's.*

HERCHEL   Cale, you watch your tongue in this church.

CALE   *(laughs)* And you watch your lustful mind 'round my gal.

> *CALE measures his brother with a look.*

Guess I got nothing to worry about. They done the job down at Beaumont. Never saw a man look so Christian glum.

HERCHEL   You been to see Daddy?

> *CALE shakes his head.*

CALE   Don't know what I could say to him. Not fixin' to come back here and play from the hymn book. You see me on TV, Herchel?

HERCHEL   I did and I swear, I thought I was watching the Wild Baboon Man from Borneo.

CALE   Liked that, did you?

HERCHEL   I guess sheep have to get lost 'fore they can get found.

CALE   Lost and real rich. Herchel, look at this, I bought Molly a little trinket. Molly, show him.

MOLLY shows him a charm bracelet.

MOLLY   The diamonds in the poodle's eyes are real and this here is a solid gold milkshake.

CALE laughs and hugs MOLLY.

CALE   I'm in love with this wild little thing, Herchel. What you think of that?

HERCHEL   You can't turn it off, can you?

HERCHEL walks away. CALE goes to him.

CALE   Herchel, you got this all wrong.

HERCHEL   Do I?

CALE   That's why we came to the church. I'm fixin' to settle down.

HERCHEL   Come on.

CALE   I'm serious, brother; Molly and me are gettin' married. *(pause)* Well, aren't you even gonna say congratulations?

HERCHEL   You're going to marry Molly?

CALE   Damn straight I am! But first there's a little wrinkle I got to iron out.

HERCHEL   What's that?

CALE   Well, as you know, Molly is but fourteen, and her daddy, he's my manager and an upright man, so I got to marry her behind his back. Thought maybe you could do that for me as a favour.

HERCHEL I can't do that, Cale.

CALE Aw come on, Herchel. Don't play cat and mouse with me. All you got to do is sign a piece of paper. I want to do this thing right, before Jesus.

MOLLY Daddy probably wouldn't mind but we don't want to take any chances.

HERCHEL You're asking me to break the law. The age of consent in this state is sixteen.

MOLLY You don't understand. We love each other!

HERCHEL Little girl, you are too young to understand even half of what Christian love and marriage is all about.

MOLLY I know Cale loves me.

HERCHEL Molly, look at him, done up like some kind of neon rooster. It's plain to see who he's mostly in love with— himself.

CALE Herchel, you got no right to judge me.

HERCHEL And you got no right to ruin this little girl's life.

MOLLY I want to get married.

HERCHEL No you don't, you're just trying to justify your sins.

MOLLY That isn't true!

CALE Hold your tongue, Herchel.

HERCHEL I am talking for Jesus.

CALE I don't believe I'm hearin' this shit!

HERCHEL And I don't believe you're pullin' this shit! I'm gonna stop it.

CALE Forget it, Herchel. I came in here to do the Christian thing and you're kickin' me out the same way Daddy did. I tell you what, we'll just shack up, that should make you real happy. Come on, Molly.

He grabs MOLLY's hand and they start to exit.

HERCHEL *(to MOLLY)* That man's gonna drag you down into the sewer, little girl. But it still isn't too late. Go home to your daddy, get down on your knees and beg for his and God's forgiveness.

MOLLY stops, confused.

MOLLY Cale, I'm afraid.

CALE You got nothing to be afraid of. I'm gonna take care of you.

CALE crosses to HERCHEL, shoves some money in his pocket and tries to give him a patronizing slap on the cheek. HERCHEL grabs his hand.

Buy Daddy some new hymn books.

HERCHEL I haven't forgotten that oath, Cale.

CALE And I ain't forgot what you said that night up on the bridge.

HERCHEL I'll bring you back to Jesus before I die. You better bet on it, boy.

CALE breaks free and drags MOLLY off.

SCENE NINE

Friday, May 29, 1959. The Brotherhood of the South lodge, Razor Back, Arkansas.

Instrumental music comes in: "The Brotherhood Of The South Anthem."

KING is standing at a podium looking very nervous. The whole community has come to hear him speak.

KING Mr. Mayor, citizens of Razor Back, friends. I want to thank you for this honour you've bestowed on me today.

VOICE Speak up, Truman, they can't hear you.

KING Sorry. I grew up in this town, and I'm proud of what Cale Blackwell is doing to bring her some fame.

> KING leads applause for CALE. Many do not applaud.

Well uh... I guess there is no denying it, I have made a
pile of money on this boy and his music, but I want to tell
you right now, I plan to do some good with it. The way
I see it, electronics is the coming thing, and I see no reason
why we shouldn't be part of it. So I put together some
backers, and I am going to build a factory right here in
Razor Back. God willing, no one 'round here is going to
ever be out of work again! So stand tall, Razor Back! Our
time to shine has come!

> KING holds his hands up over his head in a victory pose,
> looking every inch the politician. The band plays "Old
> Time Religion" instrumental underneath.

SCENE TEN

> Sunday night, August 11, 1960. The kitchen, Blackwood
> Manor, Memphis, Tennessee.

> MOLLY is at the kitchen table smoking. She's dressed up
> in a very frilly party dress. HERCHEL, on the radio, is
> underscored by a soft instrumental version of "Angel
> Band."

HERCHEL   Welcome to *The Old Time Gospel Hour.* This is the
Reverend Herchel Blackwell bringing you the good news
of the Lord Jesus Christ and his message of love and
redemption. Hallelujah.

> MOLLY doesn't notice KING walk in.

KING   Where's Cale?

MOLLY   Guess you'd know that better than me, all I do is wait
around here while you work him to death.

KING   Work him to death? I'm lucky if he's sober enough to
make the few bookings I can still get.

MOLLY   He's just tired, Daddy.

KING   He is not tired, he's plain evil. Now you tell him to come
down here, we've got to talk.

MOLLY   He's in Des Moines.

KING   Look Molly, he has not made a concert in five days.
I know he's here.

MOLLY   Daddy, I haven't seen him in six weeks.

KING   He's dragging you down, Molly. (*no reply*) Why don't you
get out. Throw some things in a bag. Come with me.

KING reaches out to take her arm. She pulls away.

MOLLY   Don't, Daddy. All you can do is stand in judgment and
criticize and that is not what I need right now.

KING   Molly—

MOLLY   No. You come down here and start pushing me around
and badmouthing him. Well, you've got no right, Daddy.
You haven't earned that kind of right with me.

KING   (*stung*) I'm pulling the plug on him. No more bookings
and not one more nickel.

MOLLY   Get the hell out!

KING   Tell him if he wants to sue me that's fine, 'cause I can
afford lawyers from now until the end of time.

*KING exits. MOLLY frantically paces, then turns the
sound back up on the radio. HERCHEL is preaching.
She sits down and listens.*

HERCHEL   (*on radio*) You in your penthouse on that top floor in that
big beautiful building in New York City. You are empty.
You are wasted inside and you know it every time you
look down from that great height and all you see are
rivers of headlights moving ceaselessly across the night…
and you know that Jesus is down there somewhere but
he's sure not in your life…

*CALE, stoned and drunk, staggers to the radio and
smashes the off button.*

CALE   What you doin' listening to Herchel's crap?

MOLLY   I wasn't. It just came on is all.

CALE   I'm goin' over to that church and kick the shit out of that bastard.

MOLLY   Cale, all I was doing was listening to the radio.

CALE   Got a date?

MOLLY   I get tired of sitting 'round here in a housecoat all day, everyday.

CALE   That so?

MOLLY   That's so. Cale, Daddy was here, he said—

CALE   Saw him outside.

MOLLY   What did you say?

CALE   I quit. Come here.

> MOLLY pushes CALE away.

MOLLY   Stop it.

CALE   What?

MOLLY   You're drunk.

CALE   I'm drunk and I'm stoned and I been up on that goddamn bus for forty-eight hours straight, now you get over here 'cause I want what I want!

MOLLY   Cale, we cannot go on living this way. We need help.

CALE   I need help? (laugh) Hell girl, you got the only thing I need, come on over here and give it to me.

MOLLY   Don't you get enough of that from those women out on the road?

CALE   On the road? Out on the road, right. Six weeks out there on a bus with every sinful sewer-bitch in the Midwest tryin' to hump the leg of my piano. You think I like that, Molly? I loathe their sinful flesh. And I love yours.

MOLLY   Don't you lie to me, Cale Blackwell. I can smell their cheap perfume from right across this room. This is all gonna stop.

> CALE flips the table. MOLLY jumps back.

CALE	Damn right. It's gonna stop, right now.
MOLLY	Cale, you're turning evil.
CALE	Evil! Since when do you talk about evil, little girl? That dog meat brother of mine poisoned your mind!
MOLLY	We got to talk to somebody, your daddy or Herchel or—
CALE	Herchel! I should have known it would turn out like this. Should have known the first time I saw you eyein' him in church.
MOLLY	What are you talking about?
CALE	You slept with him yet?
MOLLY	You're crazy.
CALE	You did, didn't you? I should have known. Look at you. You had slut in you the day you was born.
MOLLY	I'm getting out of here.
CALE	The hell you are, you whore.

He slams her to the floor.

MOLLY	You're the only man I ever been with in my whole life!
CALE	Bullshit! I can smell Herchel's pious breath all over you.

MOLLY gets up and runs out of the room. CALE follows. Offstage MOLLY screams as CALE beats on her.

SCENE ELEVEN

Monday, August 12, 1960. The Assembly of God Church, Razor Back, Arkansas.

HERCHEL is sitting at the piano practising. As he sings "Angel Band," MOLLY walks in. She wears a scarf over her hair and sunglasses. MOLLY kneels and listens to HERCHEL play.

HERCHEL	*Oh give my longing heart to him* *Who lived and died for me*

Whose blood now cleanses all from sin
And leads to victory

Oh come angel band
Come and around me stand
Bear me away on your snow white wings
To my immortal home

To my immortal home

MOLLY   You're singing good, Herchel.

HERCHEL   Long time since you've been in here listening to me. *(pauses, not sure what to say)* How's Cale doing, Molly?

> *MOLLY doesn't answer.*

Seems like these days I know a lot more about my saviour than I do my brother.

MOLLY   I'm so scared for him, Herchel.

> *MOLLY steps forward into the full light. HERCHEL realizes she's been hurt.*

He's drunk all the time and doin' pills and women. Last night he—

> *MOLLY sobs. HERCHEL moves to comfort her. He tries to take off her sunglasses. She stops him.*

HERCHEL   Molly, what did he do to you?

MOLLY   He whooped me and smashed up the house and... I left him, Herchel.

HERCHEL   There is nothing you can do but get away from that man, Molly.

MOLLY   But I love him.

HERCHEL   I love him too, but sometimes human love just isn't enough. *(pause)* There's only one person who can help you, Molly.

MOLLY   I know.

HERCHEL   Did you come here to talk to Him?

MOLLY   I did. But I'm terrible afraid.

HERCHEL   Molly, you just got to open up your heart to Him. He will come to you. He'll come into your heart, and your sins will be forgiven and you will be born again in the Lord. Won't you take Him into your heart?

MOLLY   I need Him, Herchel. I truly do.

HERCHEL   Then do it—right now. Come and pray, Molly.

>   *MOLLY takes HERCHEL's hand. They kneel at the altar together.*

MOLLY   I been tryin' to pray, Herchel, but I… I can't do it right anymore.

HERCHEL   There's no right way. You just feel it.

MOLLY   But I'm so far away from Him now.

HERCHEL   Close your eyes, Molly. Now, call Him. Reach out to Him.

MOLLY   I can't do it alone. You got to help me.

HERCHEL   Molly, you remember that old illustrated Bible of yours?

MOLLY   I remember.

HERCHEL   Remember how we used to sit on the steps of the church poring over the pictures?

MOLLY   And I'd tell you stories about Jesus.

HERCHEL   Can you tell me about one of those pictures again, Molly?

MOLLY   I—I think so.

HERCHEL   Then do, Molly, close your eyes, open your heart to Jesus and tell me about one of those pictures.

MOLLY   There was this one… a garden full of flowers in all the colours of the rainbow. And you can just tell by lookin' that the air is thick with perfume. And off in the distance there's a towering mountain of cloud standing in the sky, with a shaft of light coming straight down from it—onto a path, and Jesus he was—

HERCHEL   That's good, Molly, that's the path, the path you got to follow.

MOLLY   It's just a picture, Herchel.

HERCHEL The picture doesn't matter, Molly. It's the feeling. You've got to find the feeling you had looking at Jesus all that time ago. Find the child who loved Jesus even though she didn't understand. It's in you, Molly. It's in your heart. Find Him in your heart. Close your eyes. Walk up that path, tell me what you see.

MOLLY I see... I see... a man.

HERCHEL Tell me about him.

MOLLY He's... he's shining.

HERCHEL Go to Him.

> *MOLLY hesitates. HERCHEL squeezes her hands.*

Go to Him, Molly. Talk to Him.

MOLLY I'm all black and blue inside my soul. I have seen things and done things that are wicked.

> *MOLLY starts to cry.*

HERCHEL Let Him forgive you, Molly.

MOLLY He can't. It's too much.

> *HERCHEL takes her by the shoulders.*

HERCHEL He wants you, Molly. He wants you to be with Him. You tell Him that you forsake Satan.

MOLLY I forsake Satan, Jesus.

HERCHEL You tell Him you want Him, the Lord Jesus Christ, as your personal saviour.

MOLLY Jesus, I want you as my saviour.

HERCHEL Hold up your arms to Jesus, Molly! Stretch out your arms to Him and open your heart! *(MOLLY obeys.)* Now, pray with me again—Lord Jesus Christ.

MOLLY Lord Jesus Christ.

HERCHEL My one true saviour.

MOLLY My one true saviour.

HERCHEL Lord God on high!

MOLLY   Lord God on high!

HERCHEL   Drive out the demons of Satan inside my soul!

MOLLY   Drive out the demons of Satan inside my soul!

HERCHEL   And come into my heart!

MOLLY   And come into my heart!

HERCHEL   Forever!

MOLLY   Forever!

> *HERCHEL takes her head in a one-handed holy-fire grip,*
> *squeezing hard on her temples.*

HERCHEL   Jesus, banish Satan from this soul. Banish Satan from this
soul. Praise JESUS!

> *HERCHEL gives one mighty squeeze and pulls his hand*
> *away. MOLLY falls into his arms.*

MOLLY   Praise Jesus. Praise Jesus. Oh, Jesus. Herchel.

The Canadian Stage Company and Citadel Theatre co-production of *Fire*. Photo by Cylla von
Tiedemann. Nicole Underhay as Molly King and Rick Roberts as Herchel Blackwell.

HERCHEL He's with you now, Molly. He's in your heart and in your soul. Praise Jesus. Praise His name on high. Praise Him with me, Molly! Forever, amen.

    HERCHEL holds MOLLY tight in his arms.

SCENE TWELVE

    Sunday night, August 31, 1960. The Assembly of God Church, Razor Back, Arkansas and Riverside Racetrack, Indianapolis, Indiana.

THE PINES *(on radio) Oh come angel band*
Come and around me stand
Bear me away on your snow white wings
To my immortal home
To my immortal home

HERCHEL *(on radio)* Friends, it's been more than a year since I first started broadcasting these special Sunday services from my father's church. Doing these shows has changed my life, because it has brought me in touch with so many of you out there, so many of you who hear the word of Jesus on these broadcasts.

    Lights up on HERCHEL broadcasting his sermon.

So many who write to me, asking that a special loved one might be included in our prayers. Well, this week I got a letter I feel I must read to you all, 'cause... well it touches me and my family in a special way. It's a letter from a Mrs. T.L. from Bainbridge, Georgia. She writes:

"Dear Reverend Blackwell,

I wonder if you could say a special prayer on your show for my daughter Becky? She is very young and I fear that her soul is in peril."

    We hear the last few bars of CALE finishing a song. Lights shift to include CALE. He is at the height of his rock-and-roll mania and headed for a fall. He's gaunt, wasted on speed and halfway through the bottle of bourbon

*sitting on the piano. CALE begins a rock-and-roll vamp
on the piano, underscoring the scene.*

CALE Whooeeee! Rock and roll! I want you to get me. I want to thump and hump and drink until it's the day after tomorrow! Want to get in that saddle and ride.

HERCHEL "I don't know where Becky is anymore, but all I have to do is close my eyes and I can see her bouncing on her daddy's knee, all freckles and joy."

CALE Whooee, I am the hardest piece of meat in rock and roll. I am rock and roll. That's my name, Cale Rock and Roll.

HERCHEL "I can honestly say that Becky did not do a bad thing in all the first thirteen years of her life, but all that begin to change when the local radio station started to play rock-and-roll music. Her daddy told her this music was of Satan, but she would not listen. It seemed nothing that we could do or say was right anymore."

CALE You want to know where rock and roll comes from? It comes from hell.

HERCHEL "Things came to a head when we discovered she was seeing a boy five years her elder who was playin' guitar in a roadhouse not far from town."

CALE Hell? You want to know what hell is? I'll tell ya what hell is...

HERCHEL "Her father went out to that roadhouse to speak to the young man, and there he found our daughter drunk and in that boy's arms."

CALE You take an acetylene torch and you turn it up till you got a nice blue flame. Kind of flame cuts through a car chassis. Then you put that flame right up against your cheek.

HERCHEL "When her father confronted him the boy sneered at him and told him in coarse language what he had been doin' with our baby."

CALE You leave it there until your flesh starts a-bubblin'. You know what I mean?

HERCHEL "I have never known my husband to do a violent thing but when he heard this boy something inside of him let go."

CALE Can you feel it?

HERCHEL "My husband beat that boy to death, Herchel."

CALE Can you feel that? That's hell!

HERCHEL "I think that Becky is in Memphis, but I know she will never come home again, because her home is gone."

HERCHEL stops reading.

CALE That flame roastin' your flesh for all eternity!

HERCHEL Rock and roll killed that boy!

CALE I am it!

HERCHEL Rock and roll is killin' the youth of this country. It's destroying minds and it is killing souls!

CALE I am that flame!

HERCHEL I pray to God to strike down this music!!

CALE I'm gonna roast your ass!

HERCHEL Stop it, Lord! Stop it now, before this whole country become unto the bubblin' cesspool of Gehenna! LET US PRAY!

CALE LET US ROCK!

CALE hits the song hard. The band kicks in. Things go wild—HERCHEL moves in the spirit—a wild dance in counterpoint to the music and punctuated with freezes in classic preaching poses. CALE rocks out, both of them white-hot. CALE sings "Gonna Burn Your Playhouse Down."

You better watch it pretty baby
Burn your playhouse down
You better watch it pretty baby
Burn your playhouse down
Start a fire in the basement
Every time we mess around

I stand up on the mountain
Lookin' out across the sea
I get excited, get ignited
You know that I can't fight it
Every time you look at me

You better watch it pretty baby
Burn your playhouse down
You better watch it pretty baby
You know I ain't nobody's clown
Start a fire in the basement
Burn your playhouse down

Like a spark starts up a wild fire
Lightning striking out of the blue
Oh I go wild, honeychild
Every time I look at you

     Break.

You better watch it pretty baby
Better turn your world around
You better watch it pretty baby
You know I ain't nobody's clown
Start a fire in the basement
Every time you mess around

Start a fire in the basement
Every time you mess around

     Song crashes to an end.

     To black.

     End of Act One.

ACT TWO

SCENE ONE

Friday afternoon, May 23, 1980. King Broadcasting, Little Rock, Arkansas.

MOLLY and the NEW PINES sing "Angel Band." HERCHEL gets ready to speak.

MOLLY & PINES   *Oh come angel band*
Come and around me stand
Oh bear me away on your snow white wings
To my immortal home
Oh bear me away on your snow white wings
To my immortal home

Oh come angel band
Come and around me stand
Oh bear me away on your snow white wings
To my immortal home
Oh bear me away on your snow white wings
To my immortal home

   They sit and watch HERCHEL.

HERCHEL Hallelujah. Oh, bear me away to my immortal home. Thank you, Molly. Thank you, ladies. Glory to God. Friends, I woke up this morning from a wonderful night's sleep. My beautiful wife made me a perfect breakfast—

MOLLY Amen.

HERCHEL *(gives her a wink)* And I got in my car and drove through the sunshine over to this studio with no clear idea *whatsoever* of what I would speak about during our time together tonight. Not a clue. Not a single, solitary thought! *(to an audience member)* You look worried. *(laughs)* You know, years ago this was the kind of situation that would fill me with blind terror—no prepared text? My God, absolute adrenaline pumping, pulse-pounding, heart-palpitating terror! *(He laughs at the memory.)*

Well friends, on the drive over here today I got to thinking about how radically things have changed since God brought me to this ministry. Thank you, Jesus. I mean, here I was getting ready to stand, alone and unprepared, in front of a television camera talking to ten million strangers… but glory be to God, *I was not afraid!* Amen and amen. I knew I didn't need a memorized speech, because everything the Lord wanted me to say was stored up right here. *(his heart)* Thank you, Lord. Because, when all is said and done, I really only have one story to tell you people, and that is the story of my own heart's journey to Jesus. And God knows there is nothing complicated about that.

My journey to Jesus did not begin until I realized—*and embraced*—the simple fact that *my main strength* as a human being was that *my heart could feel pain. (pause)* I'm going to say that again. The power of the Lord did not fully enter my life until I *accepted* the fact that my greatest strength as a human being was that my heart had the *capacity* to feel pain. Do you understand what I'm saying? I opened my heart to the pain of this world! That is glorious! That is beautiful! That is God in action!

Think about it. I wasn't a great genius! I couldn't play complicated piano concertos at age four like Mr. Mozart— still can't. I did not excel in grade-school academia. I was a mediocre athlete. Like the majority of you here tonight, and like most of you watching by television, I was just a plain, ordinary, off-the-rack human being who was alone and confused by my overpowering feelings for this world. *(pause)* I felt the pain. *(pause)* I felt the pain.

Praise Jesus, I just want to say right here, right now, to all you people out there who are built like that, well, glory be to God, I think we got off lucky! Did you hear that Split Foot? *(He stamps the stage.)* I think we came out lucky! Because to live fully in this world, you've got to open up your heart and keep it open! You've got to feel the pain and you've got to care passionately about the sorrow and the suffering and the unknowable grief of your fellow man! Because, my friends, that is the only way you are ever going to be released from that pain and suffering yourself.

And that, as I stand here before you tonight, is my simple message. That's it. No, no, no, that's it, that's all! Glory to God, hallelujah! That's all we've got to do. Open up our hearts. Let Jesus in. He can feel you feeling it and HE LOVES YOU FOR IT! Open up your heart, ma'am, and let Him come in. Open up your heart, sir, and let Him come in. Open up your hearts and let Him come in!

You don't have to memorize the Bible. You don't have to burn your body. You don't have to go to Sunday school. You don't have to remember my name. You don't have to like this show. I don't care if you ever watch it again. Okay, now, I'm teasin', no, no that is the truth! That is the truth. You don't have to do anything, but open up your heart to Him. Call out to Him and He will answer! Reach out to Him and He will take your hand!

> Underscoring in. A Bach fugue played on the piano, building in intensity with the speech.

Jesus will come to you. His light will wash over you and He will heal you and He will purify you and He will lift you up and redeem you and break the bonds and set you free!

Hallelujah, hallelujah, now that is a miracle. That's a miracle—that is a miracle.

PINES   (singing) Bright morning stars

HERCHEL   Whooee! Please forgive my exuberance, I would love to be more calm and, controlled and if I was talking about Miss Gina Lollobrigida, maybe I could be, but when I talk about Jesus, so help me, I cannot contain myself!

PINES   Bright morning stars

HERCHEL   I am sayin' the light of Jesus is locked up inside of you. His light. The divine light. Open your hearts and I give you Jesus.

I give you Jesus. I give you Jesus.

Jesus saves. Jesus heals.

Jesus purifies. Jesus performs miracles.

And Jesus is coming again!

MOLLY & PINES   *Morning stars*
Morning stars
Morning stars rising
Morning stars

Bright morning stars
Bright morning stars
Bright stars are rising
Bright stars are rising
Bright morning stars
Bright morning stars
Day is breaking in my heart

MOLLY	**PINES**
Oh where	*Oh bright*
Are our—	*Oh bright*
Dear brothers	*Bright morning stars—*
Oh where	*Oh bright*
Are our	*Oh bright*
Dear sisters	*Stars*
They're gone	*Oh bright*
To heaven	*Oh bright*
The sheltered	*Bright morning stars*

ALL   *Oh day is breaking in my soul*

MOLLY	**PINES**
Oh where are our dear fathers	*Bright morning—stars are rising now*
	Bright morning—stars are rising now
Oh where are our dear mothers	*Bright morning stars are rising*
	Bright morning stars are rising
	Bright morning stars are rising
They are gone to heaven a-singing	*Bright morning stars are rising now*
	Bright morning stars are rising
	Bright morning stars are rising

ALL   (*slow*) *Oh day is breaking in my soul*

> MOLLY *and* HERCHEL *end the song in a warm embrace.*

SCENE TWO

> *Friday afternoon, May 23, 1980. Rehearsal hall, Little Rock, Arkansas.*
>
> *Sound effect: canned track of music, cheering and applause.* KING *is standing in front of an imaginary camera with a pasted-on grin and a glazed expression.* SAM, *an oily Yankee, chomps noisily on an apple.* KING *has a hard time concentrating.*

KING   I am a proud man. I am proud to be an American. I am proud to be a Southerner...

SAM   Cut! Cut! Cut the damn sound! (*to* KING) Eyeballs! Eyeballs, right?

KING   I was looking past the camera, like you told me.

SAM   Mr. King, you were squinting into the next county. If you want America to believe you, then you have to open your eyes and focus. Okay, let's try it again. (*canned sound returns*) No, no! Forget the sound! Mr. King—

KING   Where was I?

SAM   Proud to be a Southerner...

KING   But... but more than anything else I am proud to be a Christian. You see, I believe that the American ship of state is about to embark on a new journey.

SAM   Course.

KING   —on a new course, and from now on Christians are going to be up there in the wheelhouse where they belong.

SAM   Don't blink.

> SAM *takes a big chomp on his apple.*

KING   Do you have to chomp on that that damn apple? It's distracting.

SAM   On the night everything in the room is going to be distracting. That Reverend Blackwell better show up.

KING   All three networks are going to be here. He'll show.

SAM   Okay then, let's see you make it work. Tempo.

KING   *(KING cranks himself up.)* We can turn this country around! We can have a booming economy! We can be the greatest power for good this planet has ever seen, but to fulfill our destiny we must first realize that we are in a battle for the very soul of this nation and there is only one way that we will win that battle. By putting a Christian government into power. And that is why I have accepted my party's nomination for the office of US senator.

SAM   All right! Bring it down. Camera two.

KING   I want to pause right now and say a personal thank you to someone who's in this room tonight.

SAM   Sincerity.

KING   *(sincere)* If my candidacy stands for anything, it's a value system that this man delivered to me from his pulpit. So, I want to bring him up right now and thank him in front of the cameras—the Reverend Herchel Blackwell!

> SAM yells, whistles and applauds, then acts out HERCHEL's entrance.

SAM   Okay! They're with you! And here comes Herchel. Get his arm! Get it up there! Oh yeah. The crowd goes wild!

> SAM drops his arms and relaxes. KING stands with his arms upraised, beaming.

KING   Well?

SAM   Excellent. You're going to rule the world. *(tosses the apple)* Have a bite.

SCENE THREE

Saturday, May 24, 1980. Lucy's Den, Union City, New Jersey.

Instrumental music comes in, the last few bars of "The Joint Is Really Rockin'."

Lights up on CALE wearing sunglasses. He's playing in a sleazy bar. A nearly empty bottle of bourbon sits on top of the piano. He loses the tempo of the song, bangs out a dissonant series of chords and stops. He finishes off the bottle and begins to play again. He's drunk and his monologue is, at times, a little disjointed.

CALE   I want you to get me. I want you to hump and thump until the day after tomorrow…. Get in the saddle—

Starts to play again. Does a glissando. Thumps keyboard.

"So Cale, where does rock and roll come from?" "Frozen-food section."

Bangs out some dissonant chords.

Satan. It belongs to him.

Does a glissando, then thumps the keyboard.

In the airport this morning… saw a newspaper with a picture of my brother on the cover. Yeah, my brother. It said, "Holiest Man in America Takes A Stand." Whoooee.

Bangs out a few chords.

Matthew 4:8: "The Devil took him up to a high place and showed him all the kingdoms of the world and he said unto Him; All these things I will give unto thee if you will but fall down and worship me."

Bangs out an ugly blues riff.

Yeah, he's workin' for my old manager now. Can I get another bottle please!

Bangs on the piano. Waitress gets him another bottle. He starts to play.

Whooee!!!! Rock and roll. "Rock and roll is killing the
youth of this country—killing minds and...." It's a space
germ. I let that thing out of my piano and the whole
world found new ways to do sex and drugs and abortion
and demon-worshippin' blasphemies don't even got a name
yet and I am damned for that. Yes sir. I fell into the flames
of my own desire. That's why I got to keep on hosing
down my interior walls.

Takes a big drink, then takes off his sunglasses.

Look at it, brother. Lady Fame done put her blowtorch on
me. I don't preach about hell. I live in it. Now she got her
finger on Herchel. Holiest man in America! You show me
a man steals his brother's woman, I'll show you a man
with the morals of a snake. Let's get to it. Swim in a little
slime.

Plays opening of Grieg's Piano Concerto in A minor.

Just kiddin'.

*CALE plays "Last Man Standin'." Backup singers
handle call and response on refrains. The song starts as
a slow blues number then goes uptempo.*

Last man standing (Last man standing)
Last man standing (Last man standing)
Still alive
That ain't no jive
Last man standin' tonight

Let me tell you sister
There's one thing I learned
(Yeah?)

Gonna play with fire
Then you're gonna end up burned
(Yeah)
I'm the last man standing
I seen the tables turn

Well I been up
I'm goin' down
Roughshod

Good God, Lord
You hear my baby
I got nothing to lose
Last man standing
Sings those tombstone blues

Black nothin's gonna get me.
Gonna hit eternity
Won't even make a ripple
That it don't mean a damn to me
Hear the train a-rollin'
Wailin' on down the track
I'm the last man standing
And I'm never comin' back

     Break.

(Last man standing) Last man rockin'
(Last man standing) Ain't just talking
Tombstone eyes
Graveyard mind
The last man standin'
Goin' home tonight

SCENE FOUR

Saturday, June 14, 1980. TV studio, King Productions, Little Rock, Arkansas.

BLACKWELL leads MOLLY and THE NEW PINES in "Come The Morning."

BLACKWELL   Come the morning. I'm goin'
I'm goin' come the dawn
Come the morning. I'm goin'
To Jesus my soul is movin' on

In darkest of nights
When there ain't no hope in sight
And you're feeling so lonesome and low
If you open your heart
The Lord will do his part
In the mornin' to heaven we'll go

Come the morning. I'm goin'
I'm goin' come the dawn
Come the morning. I'm goin'
Sweet Jesus my soul is movin' on

On the highest of heights
In the brightest of lights
I'll stand by my sweet saviour's throne
And sing his praises high
We're all goin' by and by
Back to our heavenly home

Come the morning. I'm goin'
I'm risin' with the dawn
Come the mornin' I'm goin'
Where my spirit never more will roam

Come the morning. I'm goin'
I'm rising with the dawn
Come the morning. I'm goin'
Sweet Jesus my soul is pressin' on
Sweet Jesus my soul is pressin' on

MOLLY   Thank you, J.D. They always sound good when you're singing.

BLACKWELL   Yeah, well I love singing for flesh and blood human beings with flesh and blood problems and sins. But I don't reckon I'll ever accommodate myself to talkin' through a pile of electronic junk. Don't trust it and I never will.

MOLLY   But Reverend, you must see the good our show is doing.

BLACKWELL   I see what I see. Look what happened to Cale. That boy was strayin' but he could have been saved... until they put him on TV and twisted him around.

MOLLY   I'm still praying he'll come back to us some day.

BLACKWELL   That's good, girl, 'cause these days most of my prayers are going out for his brother.

MOLLY   J.D. Blackwell! There is more good in Herchel than there is in all of Arkansas.

BLACKWELL   For all his good that boy has a lot of pride inside him, same as his daddy. Getting so he'll do anything puts him in front of a camera. You see it too, don't ya?

> *MOLLY looks away.*

I failed 'em both all along the way. See, I raised 'em alone and a man alone is incomplete. He just doesn't have everything his children are going to need.

MOLLY   J.D., your fathering set an example for the whole community.

BLACKWELL   I tried, but a woman, she's got a power a man can never know. A way of holding a mirror up to him, makes him see beyond himself. Neither one of them got any of that until you came along. You understand what I'm saying, don't you, Molly?

MOLLY   Yes, I think I do.

> *HERCHEL and KING enter in an elated mood.*

KING   I just wish to God you could have been there, Herchel. I'll tell ya, he's not likely to come campaigning down this way in the state again. And it's all your doing, boy.

HERCHEL   Aw, now Truman. *(sees his father)* Hi Reverend! How are you feeling today?

BLACKWELL   Poorly, boy.

KING   Well sir, you would be feeling better if you had seen the work I did for the Lord this morning. I debated with the high and mighty Senator Jefferies.

Called the wrath of God down on him, I did. You wouldn't have believed it, Molly. It was glorious! Five hundred Christians with placards reading "Baby Killers Out Of Office"! Whooee!

MOLLY   But on TV he said he was against abortion.

KING   That's what he says, but just look at how he voted on the Right to Life Amendment. He's lyin' through his teeth.

BLACKWELL   I have known Jim Jefferies for fifteen years, never agreed with him on anything, but that man is not a liar.

HERCHEL   Well, Daddy I guess there's a lot of folks don't agree with you on that one.

BLACKWELL   Must say that don't surprise me if they were on your mailing list and got one of these. *(hauls out a pamphlet and reads from it)* "Your vote helped elect Jim Jefferies and in the last four years one hundred and twenty thousand unborn babies were murdered. Don't make the same mistake again." You think sending out that kind of trash is part of God's work, son?

HERCHEL   *(looks at the pamphlet)* Truman, there's a picture of us here on the back.

KING   They didn't go out as part of the ministry. *(points out a name on the pamphlet)* See, it's from the Friends of American Enterprise.

HERCHEL   Then why is my picture on the back?

KING   The picture was taken at that press conference. *(to BLACKWELL)* Neither of us approved it, Reverend.

BLACKWELL   Truman, you are starting to sound like a Yankee lawyer.

KING   All we ever did was trade mailing lists with them.

BLACKWELL   Why?

KING   J.D. We are fighting a battle for the soul of this country. Jefferies is a godless atheist and—

BLACKWELL   Well, that is another blasted lie. The man's a devout Episcopalian.

MOLLY   Daddy… if this thing isn't the truth…

KING   If you'll just listen to reason, J.D.….

BLACKWELL   What I am tryin' to do, Truman King, is find out how my son feels about sending Christians this kind of political filth!

HERCHEL   I didn't see any harm in lending our mailing list to a faith-based organization who—

BLACKWELL   Herchel, are you forgetting the Eighth Commandment of God? Thou shalt not bear false witness against thy fellow man!

HERCHEL   I had nothing to do with this... if they made a mistake.

BLACKWELL   "Thou shalt not bear false witness." That's what it says. That's what it means. It doesn't say, "Except if the man don't believe the same as you."

HERCHEL   You aren't listening to me, Daddy.

BLACKWELL   A lie is a lie, Herchel.

HERCHEL   How can you stand there and not hear a word I am saying?

BLACKWELL   There's souls out there need savin' and you are getting involved with men who are preachin' hate. Hate, plain and simple.

HERCHEL   Daddy, please...

BLACKWELL   Your brother has done a lot of sinful things in his life, Herchel, but he never called lying the will of God.

HERCHEL   Don't you go comparing me and Cale. That boy chose hell a long time ago and—

BLACKWELL   "Judge not lest you be judged." Matthew 7:1.

HERCHEL   If you will just stop for a second—

BLACKWELL   And you know what else Matthew says about what you are doing to our faith?

HERCHEL   No, what?

BLACKWELL   "Do not give what is Holy to dogs."

HERCHEL   Right.

BLACKWELL   "Neither throw your pearls before swine that they may trample them under their feet and turn around and rip you open." (*exiting*) Chapter 6, verse 6.

HERCHEL Daddy! Daddy come back—damn it, that old man doesn't understand nothing.

MOLLY Herchel!

HERCHEL I've been trying to please that man all my life. Nothing I have done amounts to anything in his eyes.

MOLLY Herchel Blackwell, your father was speaking from his heart.

Herchel, you don't think sponsoring those pamphlets is right.

HERCHEL They are from the Friends of American Enterprise, not my church!

MOLLY Well, if your own daddy can't tell the difference, you think anybody else will?

HERCHEL (glares at KING) Don't you worry, Molly, it will never happen again.

MOLLY Well then, I think you better go and tell your father that.

HERCHEL I will, but I can tell you right now, he will not listen. (exits)

MOLLY Daddy, what in God's name do you think you're doing?

KING I am trying to get elected.

MOLLY You can't use Jesus to justify lies.

KING They are not lies. They are political simplifications. You think the other side doesn't simplify and distort what I stand for?

MOLLY You are tearin' this family apart, Daddy.

MOLLY exits and KING follows.

SCENE FIVE

Monday, June 23, 1980. The municipal jail, Dallas, Texas.

CALE is curled up in a ball on a cot trying to sleep off a gigantic binge. He is being watched by JACKSON,

*a calm-eyed lunatic in perfectly pressed prison garb with
all the buttons done up. He strums a beat-up guitar and
sings off-key: "The Prison Song."*

JACKSON *Oh Mother I'm writing from prison*
I'm sorry that I've gone so wrong
The wild life done took me and broke me
Now all I have left is this song

I'm sorry if your heart is breakin'
And I'm prayin' to God high above
That he will look down and forgive me
Like you will with your precious love

CALE *(coming to)* Shut up!

JACKSON They said you were on some kind of drug withdrawal.
Are you withdrawn yet?

CALE *(sits up)* Where in hell am I?

JACKSON The prison infirmary. I'm a trustee. They give me all the
ODs and dry-outs.

CALE Lucky me. What'd I do?

JACKSON It involved a .357 Magnum.

> *CALE doesn't remember.*

You damaged a religious facility.

CALE I seem to remember this big golden cross.

JACKSON You blew it off the top of the steeple.

CALE Lucky shot.

JACKSON People are very upset.

> *A pause as CALE digests the news.*

CALE What are you in here for?

JACKSON I have a rare blood disorder.

> *CALE does a doubletake as JACKSON paces.*

If you're sick enough and there's no known cure, they just
stick you away somewhere.

CALE   What kind of blood disease?

JACKSON It's not a disease. It's a disorder. My blood supply is con-taminated by particles containing genetic material from other human beings. It's a special kind of corpuscle, kind of dimply, like a potato, and there's a tiny human face on it. An ancestor face, if you follow what I mean.

CALE   You lost me back at the dimply thing. You're not wound too tight, are you?

JACKSON Not wound too tight?

CALE   I mean, people floating around in your blood, I'm not ready for it, okay? I'm coming down off Demerol, Jack, I'm not ready for this shit.

JACKSON Nobody's ready for it. I'm not ready for it. You think I like to feel them moving around under my skin? There's one in particular, an ancient brother... he won't leave me alone. (*showing his arm*) See, I cut myself here, to let him out, but he won't come out. He likes to stay in there and give me visions. You ever get visions?

CALE   I think I'm having one right now.

JACKSON He makes trouble for me.

CALE   What kind of trouble?

JACKSON He sets fires.

> As they speak, MOLLY enters. She wears a shapeless gabardine coat, head scarf and sunglasses. JACKSON sees her, but CALE is unaware.

CALE   Listen, I heard enough, okay? I understand where you're coming from.

JACKSON Will you tell them? They pretend not to understand.

CALE   Yeah. I'll tell them.

JACKSON Good, then I'll let you see your visitor.

> JACKSON nods in MOLLY's direction then goes and sits on his cot. CALE is stunned.

CALE   Somebody die?

MOLLY	No, Cale, no one has died. *(taking off glasses)* There was a lot of press outside.
CALE	Oh. Yeah, I guess this must be a major bummer for the holiest man in America.
MOLLY	Herchel doesn't know I'm here. He probably won't like it when he finds out.
CALE	Then what are you doing here?
MOLLY	I want you to come home.
CALE	Now, where would that be?

MOLLY stares at him. CALE looks away.

MOLLY	Aw, Cale, why do you have to keep on hurting yourself?
CALE	Hurting myself? All I did was get a little drunk, okay? Pills and so on. Just flaring off some excess emotion.
MOLLY	Shooting at a cross.
CALE	They shouldn't ring 'em in neon. Makes a fat target.
MOLLY	It said in the newspaper you were naked.
CALE	A man's got the right to be naked in the privacy of his own vehicle.

CALE laughs. MOLLY doesn't.

MOLLY	Cale, every time you strike out at the world you're just trying to fight off the Lord.
CALE	Bullshit.
MOLLY	I know how it is inside you. I've been there. I know what you're made of.
CALE	Boiling pain... and that is none of your business anymore.
MOLLY	That's my choice to make.
CALE	Choice? You made your choice long ago, sweetheart. Got carried away by a sanctimonious preacher who had a hard-on for you big as a baby's arm.
MOLLY	I won't hear talk like that.

CALE   There's a lot of things you won't hear. You won't hear your daddy when he's up on TV praying to the Lord and in the next breath cozying up to those good ol' boys who own the missile factories.

MOLLY   We weren't talking about my daddy.

CALE   That's right. We were talking about Herchel. Herchel's a piece of cardboard with a smiley button for a brain.

MOLLY   Shut up.

CALE   One freedom I've got is the freedom to say what's true. I can't stand you loving him. It gives me a puke taste at the back of my mouth every time I see you on that show. I know how I used to make you feel. I know I could make you feel that way again...

He kisses her hard on the mouth. She pulls away and slaps him. JACKSON moves towards them.

MOLLY   I've been wasting my prayers on you, Cale. *(exits)* I paid the bail.

CALE   Fine. Tell those reporters out there I'll be right down! I got a story they're gonna love! About sharing blood.

CALE holds up his scarred thumb, then turns to see JACKSON staring at him.

JACKSON   You've got it too.

SCENE SIX

Sunday afternoon, June 27, 1980. King Productions, Little Rock, Arkansas.

There is a flurry of activity as the studio is set up for HERCHEL's show. Chairs are brought on and set up. MOLLY and HERCHEL enter. There's a chill between them. He prepares to speak.

PRODUCER   *(off)* Come on, come on, let's move it, get those chairs up there. We've been playing catchup all day, sleepwalking on the floor, wasting the reverend's studio time. Let's

get set up. Positions. Roll tape. Ready, Reverend. Camera
one in five, four, three, two...

HERCHEL Friends, when I look about me today I see this once-
proud nation of ours crumbling into the dust, and the reason that our nation is falling is that we are locking Jesus
out of the highest offices in this land. You say to me,
"Brother Blackwell, how did we get into this godless
mess?" Well, you know what I think? I'll tell you what
I think. I think that outside the evangelical movement the
people of this country have been deceived!

God help us, modern church theology has come to be a
kind of dainty religious mush that's got more to do with
John Lennon than it's got to do with St. John the Divine.

Jesus said, in John, Chapter 14, verse 6, "I am the Way
and the Truth and the Life. No one comes to the Father
except through me." No one comes to the Father except
through me. These modern churches are saying, "I am the
way." The secular humanists who, God help us, are running
this country are saying, "No, no, *I am the way.*" Well, I am
here to tell you that they are wrong! The modern churches
are wrong! The government is wrong!

They're all wrong 'cause I'll tell you, there is only one
Truth, glory be to God, and that Truth is in the Holy
Bible. God's word: "I am the Way. I am the Truth. No one
comes to the Father except through me!" That's what he
told us in the book!

And if we're... if we're going to save this crumbling nation and
save our souls then we need men in government who believe
that, people. We've had enough of these men who say, "I am the
way. My will be done." We need men who say, "He is the Way.
His will be done!"

It's simple enough. I think what we have to ask ourselves
is this, "Are the men taking the will of the people to
Washington Christian men? Will they serve the will of
God in government?" If we ask that question of our
candidates and let the good Lord guide our consciences,
then, praise Jesus, we will turn this rotting, sinful world

around. And if we don't? If we don't, then as sure as this *(holds up Bible)* is the Word of God. As sure as this is the living word of God, the forces of evil that surround us will prevail and we will burn in hellfire forever. You think on that. Molly—

> *The intro for "Poor Wayfaring Stranger" begins.*
> *MOLLY walks forward preparing to sing as the cameras*
> *shift focus to her.*

MOLLY   *I am a poor wayfaring stranger*
While travelling through this world of woe
But there's no sickness nor toil nor danger
In that bright land to which I go

I'm going there to see my brother
The Lord will greet me when I come
I'm only going over Jordan
I'm only going to my home.

> *MOLLY falters.*

I—I'm sorry... can we...

> *MOLLY breaks down. HERCHEL moves to her.*

HERCHEL   Molly, you all right?

MOLLY   No... I can't... my God, there I am singing that song... and... why are you acting as if nothing's wrong? Why don't you just get angry and get it over with?

PRODUCER   *(off)* Stop tape.

HERCHEL   I'm not angry! *(pause)* There's not a whole lot to say, is there? You went to see him. Your heart was in the right place, I suppose, but it was a huge mistake for you to get involved.

MOLLY   No, Herchel...

> *Stagehands begin to work around the set. HERCHEL,*
> *hyper-aware of them, speaks softly.*

HERCHEL   Molly, it's not a good idea to try and talk about this right now. *(whispers)* Do you have any idea how it makes me feel to see that man drag you through the mud?

MOLLY   Yes, I think I do.

HERCHEL   No, I don't think that you do.

PRODUCER   *(off)* Reverend?

HERCHEL   Just a minute, Andy. *(to MOLLY)* I'm not going to tell you I don't feel anger, but I can take care of that myself.

MOLLY   No, Herchel, you can't, I mean, if you could have heard that sermon you just delivered. I never thought you'd be talking like that on this show.

HERCHEL   Like what?

MOLLY   Like one of my father's speechwriters.

HERCHEL   You think I'm wrong?

MOLLY   I don't know. The Jesus I saw in your heart and the stuff you're talking about are—

HERCHEL   Molly, we can't choose where Jesus will lead us, we can only follow. I believe I'm doing God's will.

MOLLY   But what if this isn't God's will? What if it's your will, or my daddy's will? What if it's like your father says, it's all just pride driving you on into God knows what?

PRODUCER   *(off)* We're getting pretty far behind, Reverend.

MOLLY   Herchel, I'm scared.

HERCHEL   Well don't be. Okay, Andy, we'll run the Family Fund tape in there and cut right to the closing.

MOLLY   I love you, Herchel.

HERCHEL   I love you too, honey.

PRODUCER   *(off)* Ready when you are, sir.

HERCHEL   Okay, let's just do this thing.

> *HERCHEL takes his mic and goes to his spot on the stage.*

PRODUCER   *(off)* Okay, quiet on the set! *Herchel Blackwell Show*, scene eight, pickup three, in five, four, three, two...

The Canadian Stage Company and Citadel Theatre co-production of *Fire*.
Photo by Cylla von Tiedemann. Ted Dykstra as Cale Blackwell.

SCENE SEVEN

1:45 a.m., Friday, June 29, 1980. Slammer's Bar, Macon, Georgia.

CALE sings "Let Me In Baby," a frantic thrashing song played at breakneck speed.

CALE
Let me in baby, please unlock the door
Let me in baby, I can't take it no more
Let me in baby, I know I'm to blame
Let me in baby, now I'm goin' insane
Come on baby, it's startin' to rain

I know I done you wrong
I know I been a fool
But honey it's cold outside
And I'm still in love with you

So let me in baby, now I'm beggin' you
Let me in baby, now I'm feelin' so blue
Let me in baby, now I'm starting to cry
Let me in baby, baby don't say goodbye
Let me in baby, I'm fixin' to die

   Break.

Come on baby, I crawled up the stairs
Come on baby now, answer my prayers
Come on baby, I know my name's in your book
Come on baby, forgive a crook
Aw baby I'm really shook
Let me in baby I'm really shook
Let me in baby I'm really shook

CALE finishes the song, grabs a bottle and slumps at a table. He doesn't see KING stalk him.

KING   Been reading about you and my little girl.

CALE   That a fact?

KING pulls the bottle out of CALE's hand.

KING   You fall on your face in public that's one thing, but dragging down the reputations of innocent people who are trying to do some good in this world is something else again.

CALE I know.

KING There are precious few people on this earth give a damn about you and she is one of them.

CALE I already gave the damn interviews, Truman. Can't do nothing about it now.

KING Try showing a little backbone.

KING hands CALE an envelope.

CALE What's this?

KING A contract. I've got a campaign telethon next week. I want you to play on it.

CALE You have got to be kidding.

KING I have never been more serious in my life. We both know Molly went to that jailhouse with your salvation in mind. Now, let's show the people of this country what that kind of faith can do.

CALE And how are "we" going to do that?

KING I want you singing gospel.

CALE You always were a crazy bastard.

KING Look, Cale, you've got a trial coming up that is going to be a media circus. It's going to hurt Molly and your brother.

CALE Yeah?

KING Okay, it will hurt my campaign, too.

CALE Ah.

KING But there is nobody it is going to hurt more than you. They're going to put you away, boy.

CALE They will never take me alive, Truman.

KING No joke, Cale. The truth of the matter is you are killing yourself. You know what you are going to leave behind?

CALE   Nothing.

KING   You are going to leave behind a family knowing that somebody they loved lived and died without ever making peace with them... or himself. This is probably your last chance to make it right. *(KING drops the contract in front of CALE.)* I don't know, maybe you don't have the stomach for it. Then again, maybe you do. Call my people if you want to talk.

> *KING exits. CALE opens the contract and begins to read.*

SCENE EIGHT

Saturday morning, July 5, 1980. King Productions, Little Rock, Arkansas.

HERCHEL is delivering a sermon.

HERCHEL   Second Peter. Chapter 3, verse 10. "But the day of the Lord will come as a thief in the night. In which the heavens shall pass away with a great noise and the elements shall melt with a fervent fire. The earth also and the works that are therein shall be burnt up."

> *MOLLY crosses the darkened edges of the studio. KING approaches her and she starts to walk away. He grabs her arm.*

KING   Molly—

MOLLY   Daddy, I've got no time—

KING   No Molly, wait. Look, I know things have been bad between us. I've made mistakes, I know that, but I can make it all right again.

MOLLY   How are you going to do that?

KING   There's somebody in the dressing room who needs to talk to you.

HERCHEL   In Revelations, St. John speaks of a great battle. A time of fire and death and resurrection for the anointed and retribution for the sinner.

MOLLY   I want no part of your plans.

KING   You've got to trust me. Trust me, and I promise I'll get us clear of this mess we're in. Okay?

KING and MOLLY exit.

HERCHEL   I tell you, this great battle between good and evil will be fought in the Holy Lands, in modern times with modern weapons. Just like St. John the Divine saw it in Revelations two thousand years ago! You think the Iranians aren't building the bomb? You think the Jews don't have one already?

SCENE NINE

Saturday morning, July 5, 1980. The makeup room, King Productions, Little Rock, Arkansas.

JAMES, the makeup man, is working on CALE.

JAMES   The eyes. The eyes are a disaster. Not nearly blissful enough.

CALE   The only one gonna do better than that is the undertaker.

JAMES   Well, I did once work for the Grateful Dead. Sweet boys. Sinful times.

CALE   No offence.

JAMES   You are going to need an inch of pancake if you expect to bamboozle the local hanging judge with this salvation crap.

CALE   Man, you got me wrong.

MOLLY   *(entering)* James, Daddy says there's somebody down here I... Cale.

CALE   Molly.

JAMES   Rhett. Scarlet.

MOLLY   *(angry)* What are you doing here?

JAMES   He is here to repent his sins, honey. *(exits)* Good luck.

MOLLY   How could you come here after what you said in those papers?

CALE   Truman wants me to go on his show and sing gospel.

MOLLY   What?

CALE   Figures maybe it will get those newspapers off your back.

MOLLY   Does Herchel know about this?

CALE   No. Look, Molly... there comes a time when even a man as blind and stupid as me realizes he's hit bottom. I don't know exactly what I'm doing, I just know I don't want to keep on hurting people. I don't expect your forgiveness, or Herchel's forgiveness, but if I just set this one thing straight maybe that's enough. I'll walk out of here if that's what you want me to do, but if you'll just give me a chance...

JAMES   *(enters)* Mr. Blackwell, time to get that handsome ruined puss before the cameras. Chop, chop. *(exits)*

MOLLY   Cale, that night at the jail...

CALE   Everything I said that night was garbage.

MOLLY   No, Cale, not all of it. Herchel *is* in trouble. He and your daddy aren't talking, and my daddy... I kept saying to myself all I've got to do is stand by him and love him, but I talk to him and he doesn't hear me anymore... I don't even know what is wrong with him.

CALE   Pride, maybe?

MOLLY   Guess you know a little about that.

CALE   I wrote the book.

MOLLY   You've got to help him.

CALE   Now, how can I get close enough to him to do that?

MOLLY   Beg his forgiveness.

CALE   Molly, it will take everything I got just to sing one song...

MOLLY That's not enough to save him or you. *(pause)* Cale, look at this scar I got on my finger. You got one, too, and so does Herchel—

CALE Don't go pitching a schoolboy oath at me, Molly.

MOLLY Who'd you and Herchel make that oath to, Cale?

CALE Jesus.

MOLLY And where is He in your life now?

CALE Don't. Don't go turning this thing into a crapshoot for my soul. I was damned long ago. Herchel knows that.

MOLLY Jesus never told anybody they were damned. He said, "Come unto me and be saved."

CALE Why should He want to save me?

MOLLY Because He loves you.

CALE I find that hard to believe.

MOLLY You always have, Cale, but it's the simple truth.

MOLLY puts her hand in CALE's and squeezes hard. He looks at her, then without saying anything, stands, still holding her hand, and walks into the studio.

SCENE TEN

Saturday, July 5, 1980. King Productions, Little Rock, Arkansas.

Song vamps under KING as he enters.

KING You know folks, when I was startin' out in the fifties there was a time when I despaired of God's love. It seemed that everything I turned my hand to—I failed at it. Then I took to managing Cale Blackwell and he made me a million dollars. He made me a million dollars, that's right, and he brought my family to ruin and darn near killed my daughter in the process. Why? Why? Because Cale Blackwell turned his face from God. He turned his face from God and embraced evil. And God took away his health and took away his fame and took away his money, but he did not take away his soul. And tonight... tonight on this special Christians for King Telethon, Cale Blackwell is coming back to Jesus!!

> *KING steps off to one side. CALE is in place at the piano. He sings "Lost Out In Deep Water."*

CALE *My sinful life has brought me here*
And turned my dreams to stone
And to tell the truth, the good Lord knows
I've reaped just what I've sown

Now, I'm a man lost in a storm
The pain's just rainin' down
I'm lost out in deep water, Lord
Oh Lord don't let me drown

I climbed the stairway to the stars
Then tumbled to the bottom
Lord I thought I was a king
But I was just a fool
I failed with you
And I failed at life
I'm lost, can I be found?
I'm lost out in deep water, Lord
Oh Lord don't let me drown

I'm downing in an ocean
Of lies and misery
Sweet Jesus, your love
Is what I need so desperately

My life it flashes by me
And with fire I am crowned
I'm lost out in deep water, Lord
Oh Lord don't let me drown
I'm lost out in deep water, Lord
God don't let me drown
Lord don't let me down

> *CALE finishes his song. There is applause. He jumps up and, excited by his success, gives MOLLY a big lift-me-up-swing-me-around hug. At that instant HERCHEL walks in.*

HERCHEL Molly!

KING comes hustling out of the control booth.

CALE Hey brother, how did it sound?

HERCHEL It sounded like hell.

KING Herchel—

HERCHEL Truman, are you out of your mind lettin' that boy in here?

KING Look Herchel, our campaign is…

HERCHEL Are you campaigning for congress or dog catcher? You put that sinner on the air and you'll be flushing your chances down the drain.

MOLLY He wants to be saved, Herchel.

HERCHEL Oh, save his soul. Is that some kind of sick joke?

CALE Now hold on, Herchel.

HERCHEL No. I know you, Cale. *(looking at MOLLY)* There's no way you're here looking for Jesus.

MOLLY Herchel—

HERCHEL Truman, you run that tape you're gonna have to find yourself a new preacher.

KING Saving him is going to get those papers off our backs, Herchel. We can make points on this boy.

MOLLY Make points? Daddy—

HERCHEL I'm telling you, Truman.

KING And I'm telling you. Cale coming back to Jesus can put me over the top and I want him on the air.

HERCHEL In that case you better start thinking about what to tell the voters of this state when they hear that I walked.

MOLLY This is crazy. Herchel, he—

HERCHEL You keep out of this, Molly. What do you say, Truman? Him or me.

CALE Herchel.

HERCHEL I have no time for—

CALE Herchel, look at me! *(pause)* You... you remember how Daddy was always makin' us memorize them Bible verses? Remember that one: "A certain man had two sons, and the younger of them... the younger of them took his journey into a far country and there wasted his... wasted himself"? Don't remember the rest.... It's Luke, right?

HERCHEL Chapter 15 and you got it all messed up.

CALE Guess 'cause I'm all messed up myself, huh?

> *HERCHEL is stone-faced.*

I ain't gonna try and trade Bible quotes with you, Herchel. You could always beat me at it... but I need you, brother... and I'm thinkin' maybe you need me from what Molly says—

HERCHEL You keep Molly out of this.

CALE Now, how am I gonna do that, man? She's been in the middle of this thing ever since the start, ever since that night on the bridge. We both know that. She loves you. Herchel? You hear me, man? She loves you... and I love you, too.

Remember our oath, Herchel? "With Jesus in the here-after, and with my brother in the here and now." We go to heaven together, or we don't go at all.

HERCHEL You smashed that oath to pieces a long time ago, Cale.

CALE I sure as hell tried, brother, but it can't be done. I want to come home. I need you... and Jesus. Now.

HERCHEL "For it is impossible as regards those who have once been enlightened and who have tasted the heavenly free gift and have partaken of the Holy Spirit... if they have fallen away, to revive them again to repentance, because they impale the Son of God afresh for themselves and expose him to public shame." You remember that one, Cale? "It is impossible to revive the fallen who have exposed Jesus to public shame." Hebrews 6:4 to 6. You erase that tape, Truman.

KING   You heard the reverend, boys, erase the tape. *(exits)*

CALE   You know what, Herchel? The Jesus you got left inside of you could dance on the head of a pin.

> *CALE pulls a flask out of his pocket, toasts MOLLY and drinks.*

I'll see y'all in hell.

> *CALE exits. MOLLY runs after him.*

MOLLY   Cale! You're wrong, Cale! Wait, Cale! Please, you're wrong!

> *HERCHEL sits, picks up his Bible and tries to read. A long beat. MOLLY re-enters.*

How could you do that?

HERCHEL   He's gone?

MOLLY   Yeah, he's gone all right. He's gone to hell.

HERCHEL   Well, praise be to God you didn't go with him.

MOLLY   You just killed that boy, same as if you ran him down with a truck.

HERCHEL   He's been trying to kill himself since Momma died. There's nothing I can do about that.

MOLLY   "Am I my brother's keeper?" Remember that one, Herchel? Genesis 4:9, "And the Lord said unto Cain, where is Abel thy brother? And he said—"

HERCHEL   I know the verse!

MOLLY   You need each other, Herchel.

HERCHEL   Look Molly, we are fast becoming the biggest gospel show on TV. I am saving ten thousand souls a night. I know I am. We can't endanger everything we built here by gambling on a man who has been wallowing in filth for twenty years.

MOLLY   Herchel, have you gone blind? Cale was on his knees reaching out to you, and you cut him down and walked away.

HERCHEL   Look, there's nobody on this planet who'd be happier to see that boy saved, and if he really wants redemption there's a half a dozen churches down on Main Street.

MOLLY   He needs your forgiveness. *(no reply)* What's happened to you? You're acting like you've lost your soul.

HERCHEL   Mind your tongue, woman!

MOLLY   The hell I will! My whole life I've been bouncing between you two searching for something that approaches a decent way to live.... I thought you had the answer, Herchel, now look at you.

HERCHEL   You shut up!

MOLLY   No Herchel, I will not shut up. Your daddy was right, all you're doing is preaching hate. I just can't go on with it. All I hear from you these days is St. John the Divine, Revelations and how all true believers are gonna be raptured up just before the Middle East gets vaporized. And there's my daddy campaigning on a Christian plat-form talking about missiles for Jesus. Is that what Jesus stood for?

HERCHEL   Jesus is my Lord and my personal saviour and I do my damnedest to be true to him. You know that, Molly.

MOLLY   All I know is that I saw your own brother on his knees begging to you, and you just turned away. I can't live with that picture in my mind, Herchel. I can't. Unless you get up this very minute and leave this building and find Cale and bring him home... I am leaving you.

HERCHEL   I got an appearance to tape on Truman's show in a half-hour and you want me to go out rummaging through the bars of this town looking for that no-account drunk? I will not do it.

MOLLY   Then I'm going.

HERCHEL   Oh fine, then you go to him. That's what you want, isn't it? You always had some Satan left inside your soul.

MOLLY   I'll pray for you, Herchel. Same way I pray for him.

MOLLY exits. Lights fade down on HERCHEL reading his Bible.

SCENE ELEVEN

Election night in Arkansas. Action shifts between KING giving his acceptance speech and MOLLY back in the church in Razor Back.

Instrumental music, "The Brotherhood Of The South Anthem," swells as KING strides to a podium.

ANNOUNCER Ladies and gentlemen, I give you our new senator for the sovereign state of Arkansas, Truman H. King!

KING Brothers and sisters! They used to talk about a silent majority in this country, but we are silent no more!! We are sending some Bible-believing men into Babylon!

Sound fades out, leaving KING frozen in a victory pose. Lights fade up on MOLLY kneeling on a chair downstage.

MOLLY Jesus, it seems like a long time since I really talked to you. But last night I was watching TV and, ah... this old Gary Cooper movie came on? *High Noon*. And it got me thinking about the old illustrated Bible my daddy gave me.

KING And we are going to kick some secular rear ends, I'll tell you.

MOLLY I went and got that old Bible out, just to look at those pictures again. But all those shining full-colour prints of the life of Jesus, they looked crude to me. I found it hard to believe that the man in those pictures had been the first love of my life.

KING Because, let me tell you friends, this nation is falling, and it is falling because of the enemy within.

MOLLY Then I started to read the words beside the pictures.

KING I'm sick of the putrid, pathetic, pukish pulp that passes for entertainment coming over our TV sets. I am sick of evolution, I am sick of secular humanism, I am sick of homosexuality!

MOLLY   I read all night..I read through the Gospel of John, and the Acts of the Apostles and I thought of those men, those real flesh and blood men who suffered from the heat and the cold and died for their love of you.

KING   So don't talk to me about the separation of church and state. You talk to me about the will of God!

MOLLY   Then I got to Corinthians. Chapter 13.

KING   You talk to me about how we are going to put God back into every home in this country!

MOLLY   "If I speak in the tongues of men and of angels but do not have love I have become a sounding brass or a clashing cymbal. And if I have the gift of prophesying and am acquainted with all the sacred secrets and all the knowledge, and if I have all the faith so as to move mountains, but do not have love, I am nothing. Love is long suffering and kind."

KING   There will be no more baby murderers in our hospitals! Truman King is going to see to that!

MOLLY   "Love is not jealous."

KING   There will to be no more filth taught in our schools. Truman King is going to see to that!

MOLLY   "It does not brag, does not get puffed up, it does not behave indecently, does not look for its own interests, does not become provoked. It does not keep account of the injury. It does not rejoice over unrighteousness, but rejoices with the truth. It bears all things."

KING   I'm going to see our courts start thinking right.

MOLLY   "Believes all things."

KING   We are going to root out evil wherever it exists.

MOLLY   "Hopes all things. Endures all things."

KING   We will build up an army for Christ. A force so fearsome our enemies will quake before this nation's might.

MOLLY   "Love never fails."

KING   And some folks may say, "Hey, Truman, ain't you afraid of starting a nuclear war?"

MOLLY   "Now however there remain faith, hope and love, these three, but the greatest of these is love." And at that moment I began to remember what love was again, and to find it in my heart.

KING   And I say to them, if it comes down to having a world without Christ, then I say blow the whole damn thing to kingdom come and send me on over into Zion!

> *Music swells. KING freezes in the classic V for Victory pose.*

MOLLY   That is how you come into the world isn't it, Jesus? You come as love. Oh Jesus, I pray you will fill the hearts of all men with your love at this time when we need it so much. Thy will be done. Amen.

> *The End*

SONG CREDITS

"Bright Morning Stars" – traditional

"Swing Down Chariot" – traditional

"Devil In Her Eyes" by Paul Ledoux

"Salvation Highway" by Paul Ledoux

"Really Rockin' Tonight" by Paul Ledoux

"Old Time Religion" – traditional

"The Brotherhood Of The South Anthem" by Paul Ledoux

"Angel Band" by William Bradbury & Jefferson Hascall – public
    domain

"Gonna Burn Your Playhouse Down" by Paul Ledoux

"Last Man Standin'" by Paul Ledoux

"Come The Morning" by Paul Ledoux

"The Prison Song" by Paul Ledoux

"Poor Wayfaring Stranger" – traditional

"Let Me In Baby" by Paul Ledoux

"Lost Out In Deep Water" by Paul Ledoux

PAUL LEDOUX is one of the most-produced creators of musical theatre in Canada. Among his thirty-seven produced plays are *Fire* (with David Young), *Dream A Little Dream: the nearly true story of The Mamas and The Papas* (with Denny Doherty), *The Secret Garden, Hot Flashes* (with John Roby), *Cheatin' Hearts* (with David Smyth), *Still Desire You* (with David Young and Melanie Doane). Current theatrical projects include *Paris before The Crash* (with John Roby), a new musical about Canadian members of The Lost Generation.

Ledoux has also written extensively for Canadian television, including *Pit Pony*, a family series for Cochran Entertainment (head writer/supervising producer), and radio, including *The Old Guy*, a mystery series for CBC (Canadian Screenwriting Award nominee).

DAVID YOUNG's theatrical works include *Love is Strange* (with Paul Ledoux); *Glenn*, a theatrical portrait of Glenn Gould, which had numerous productions in Canada (including at the Stratford Festival) and overseas and *Inexpressible Island*, which was produced in Canada, the United States, Germany and London's West End. Both *Glenn* and *Inexpressible Island* were nominated for the Governor General's Literary Award. *Clout*, a portrait of a neoconservative press baron, was co-produced by the National Arts Centre and Tarragon Theatre. David

also wrote an adaptation of Ibsen's *An Enemy of the People* and has adapted Alistair MacLeod's award-winning novel *No Great Mischief* for Tarragon Theatre. Current theatrical projects include *Without Hope, Without Fear*, a theatrical portrait of Caravaggio for the NAC.